Song of the Solipsistic One

Deepa Majumdar

The Prometheus Trust

The Prometheus Trust
28 Petticoat Lane
Dilton Marsh, Westbury
Wiltshire, BA13 4DG, UK

A registered charity, number 299648

Song of the Solipsistic One

Deepa Majumdar

2013

ISBN 978 1 898910 633

British Library Cataloguing-in-Publication Data.
A catalogue record for this book is
available from the British Library.

Printed in the UK by Berforts Information Press, King's Lynn

Dedication

This work is dedicated to the Holy Mother, Sri Sarada Devi (1853-1920), wife and spiritual consort of Sri Ramakrishna (1836-1886).

Song of the Solipsistic One

TABLE OF CONTENTS

Introduction

In these times, it is perhaps best for an author to "confess" her sources of inspiration and influence. Certainly, no work of science or art arises in a vacuum. Not only the work of science, but also the poetic work is rooted in empirical reality. In fact, all works of art are rooted in basic worldviews *of* empirical reality ... *weltanschauungs* that draw *from* the same reality. A work of art uses sensory images delivered by the power of fancy. To construct these images ... even if mere shapes ... imagination uses a basic alphabet ... hieroglyphs drawn *from* empirical reality, understood as corporeal nature.[1] Nevertheless, there is, I believe, in all acts of creativity, a place for the interior life. That moment when we conjure *this* work of art ... but more so, that moment of quiet inspiration that precedes conception ... when we receive this work, in a state akin to revelation ... these hallowed moments belong exclusively to the interior life ... Entirely inward, these moments are detached from empirical reality.

My influences are many, but my inspiration remains the perennial, universal mystic vision of oneness. I admire greatly the depth of thought in the works of western thinkers like Plato (BC 427-347), Plotinus (AD 204/5–270), William Wordsworth (1770-1850), Emily Brontë (1818-1848) and Bertrand Russell (1872-1970). They have helped me evolve in my thinking and writing. But my ultimate inspiration comes from the great sages and poet seers of the Indian tradition, whose highest trans-discursive experiences have shaped the basic vision of Advaita Vedanta. My work is rooted in a consistent existential-theological-metaphysical paradigm drawn from this Advaitic vision, which differs in significant ways from the worldviews of Plato and Plotinus.

This basic non-dual vision, the most radical monism ever, asserts that there is, in the end, only one Reality – namely God (*Brahman*). Inasmuch as this solitary Reality is the universal Self – a supreme object-free Subject – it becomes the *solipsistic* One. When this Reality enters human history ... that is, when the Infinite appears in the guise of the finite ... it comes in the form of the Divine Incarnation or

---

[1] In his *First Meditation*, René Descartes points out that imagination is grounded in corporeal nature. I make the same case here. Unlike Descartes, I take empirical reality, as such, to extend beyond corporeal nature to include the places of afterlife, subject to Time and *Maya* ... But in this sentence, I use empirical reality to mean only corporeal nature.

Avatara. It is this Reality that creates and sustains the empirical worlds, quite as a desert sustains the mirage it supports on itself.[2] In contradistinction with the Real, which is Absolute, the created worlds have a mere *relative* existence. They derive their reality from the Real. Bereft of their Divine Substratum, they are *unreal*, or illusory. Nevertheless, this One Reality is not remote from the multiplicity it creates. Letting itself be limited by each of the limiting adjuncts of the many, this One *appears* as the many. For the One is the essence underlying the limiting adjuncts that constitute the *appearance* that is multiplicity – an appearance conjured by the divine power of *Maya*. In short, it is these unreal limiting adjuncts that constitute the Cosmic Illusion conjured by *Maya*. Reality, or Existence-Knowledge-Bliss Absolute (*Sachchidānanda*) transcends the moral sphere so that it is *beyond* good and evil, even as it serves as the supra-moral Substratum of good and evil. Goodness is valuable, not in itself, but in the expiatory power it possesses to exhaust evil. Vedantic thought differs from western thought in *these* aspects ... that Divine Reality transcends the pairs of opposites ... even as it is immanent in this domain of *Maya*; that the pairs of opposites that pervade the thralldom of *Maya* include this momentous pair ... namely, good and evil; that Divinity is Truth itself ... so that Truth too is transcendent *and* immanent; that Truth therefore surpasses all pairs of opposites, including good and evil, even as it serves as the only Real substratum of all unreal becoming; that the Divine therefore exceeds goodness, for it is supra-moral.[3]

In this work, I envision the Divine, poetically, as a magnificent Sun ... coiling round and round ... animated by the twin powers of contemplation and aspiration. Our human prayers and meditation rotate this flaming wheel. But the whirling Sun, in turn, attracts to itself "thought lanterns" from the human mind. It serves as the womb of purified thought, but also as the destination of purified thought. It is therefore the Sun of Divine Love. There are, I believe, running threads of thought that connect the different historical manifestations and

[2] I borrow this metaphor of the desert and its mirage from Swami Nikhilananda who says, "Just as a mirage cannot be seen without the desert, which is its unrelated substratum, so also the universe cannot exist without Brahman." See "Discussion of Brahman in the Upanishads," in *The Upanishads, A New Translation*, by Swami Nikhilananda, vol I (New York: Ramakrishna-Vivekananda Center, 1990), 37.

[3] One exception is the "Table of Opposites" ascribed to Pythagoras. As described by Aristotle the ten opposites in this table include "Good" and "Bad."

permutations of the collective consciousness ... linking them across the chasm of history ... tying the overall Spirit of History into a seamless whole. Ancient ideas with truth value, appear and reappear in this historical flow of the common consciousness. Each serves its special historical purpose. Solar theology, which was not uncommon in ancient thought systems, therefore deserves a place in our present day common consciousness.

On the afterlife, I have retained the basic eastern notion that the heavens and hells are graded in tiers. Both are subject to Time. Both fall under the domain of *Maya*. Both are therefore part of the Cosmic Illusion. Time is simply the opposite of Eternity. It is not a copy of Eternity. Inasmuch as *Brahman* is eternal, Eternity is Real, whereas Time is unreal. I have also retained the basics of Vedantic cosmology ... that there are multiple appearances and disappearances of the universe. Or, to use the poetic words of Sri Ramakrishna (1836-1886) ... there are as many universes as there are grains of sand. The domain subject to *Maya* is ruled by five existential paradigms – Time, Space, Becoming, Causality, Death. I use "Chief Sentinels" to characterize the following paradigms (some of them existential) – Time, Death, Desire, Good, Evil (Poem 45). Escape from, or transcendence of *Maya* calls for an ethical journey that garners enough good to exhaust all evil acquired in the multitude of lives that have led to the current life. The journey of transmigration is inherently moral (in its purpose), entailing multiple lifespans, each immersed in Time. From its roost beyond good and evil, the one Reality engaged in its divine sport, or *Lila*, attracts all created beings. Human consciousness is capable of responding ethically to this call, for the further purpose of reaching the ultimate salvific goal of *Brahma-Nirvana*. In this awakening in *Brahman* ... in this act of final Self-knowledge ... we experience a unitive knowing of ourselves as the one universal Self, or the one Reality that is *Brahman*. All acts of knowing *unite* knowers with their objects of knowledge. But the seeming "union" here is more a revelation of the hallowed object of knowledge. For this Self-knowing is really an *actualization* of (not union with) the concealed universal Self. This teleological highest Self is ever potential in each being, but it is capable of being consciously kindled only in man and in celestial beings. I therefore use the upper case "S" for "Self-knowledge" ... because the object of this knowing is not the immanent lower self ... but the highest universal solitary transcendent-immanent divine "Self" or *Atman* (*Brahman* in each being). *Brahma-Nirvana* is therefore a recovery of the true, eternal Self, which is a seeming substratum of the fleeting seeming selves that flow through the cycle of reincarnation. All reincarnation stops once the trans-temporal experience of *Brahma-Nirvana* ensues.

I have retained some Sanskrit terms.[4] *Brahman* (static God) means Supreme Absolute Reality. *Brahman* manifests its immanence through its "personal" limiting adjunct of *Maya*, which serves as the grand prism that appears to break the solipsism of the One into a prismatic, phantasmal many. But this is only seeming, for in the end ... *Brahman* alone abides. *Maya*, the inscrutable dynamic power of God (identical with *Brahman*), is projected by the static God to create the empirical worlds. *Maya* is also the "ignorance obscuring the vision of God." It is the "Cosmic Illusion that causes the One to appear as the many, the Absolute as the Relative." *Maya* therefore seeks to obscure the Real from created beings, thus tethering them to the unenlightened state. "*Aum*," the quintessential sacred syllable (not word) is *Brahman* in sonic form. It is that primordial sound, which I refer to as the "soundless sound," "Divine Hum," "Song of the *Logos*," "Simple Song," etc. It is that original sound from which all sounds are distilled. *Karma* is "action in general," or duty, while the Law of *Karma*, a transcendental law that might be described, in its applications, as a Dynamic Judgment Day, metes out rewards and punishments. It is a "law of cause and effect" that leads each action to its morally appropriate *triple* effects. Every action leads first, to the merit or demerit it earns through that action ... second, to the *karmic* reward or punishment fetched by that action ... third, to a subsequent action that follows as a morally logical consequence of the first. This law applies only to beings with free will or beings who *can* be culpable – that is, to human persons and celestial beings. Inasmuch as this law operates within the thralldom of *Maya*, it applies not only to rational beings in corporeal nature, but also to those in the places of afterlife and in the celestial domains of gods and deities. "*Karmic* ledger" is a term I coin to depict the account of merit and demerit that trails each human person through his/her unique trajectory of reincarnation. Finally, *Mantra* is a "sacred word or mystic syllable in Sanskrit" used in the repetitive prayer (*japam*) taught by *Guru* (spiritual Preceptor) to disciple. I have drawn *Mantric* as an adjective from the noun *Mantra*.

In this paradigm, the ego bound notion of "soul" is somewhat inappropriate. For "soul," with its constancy of individuality, simply

[4] All basic definitions and quotes (unless otherwise cited) are taken from Swami Adiswarananda, *Meditation and its Practices: A Definitive Guide to Techniques and Traditions of Meditation in Yoga and Vedanta* (Woodstock: Skylight Paths Publishing, 2003), 453-460.

does not accommodate the conception of multiple domino-like lower selves, each, a transient state of being, replete with *karmic* activity. Nevertheless, I have used "soul" in some poems. What I meant was a temporary identity. But the picture of the self I envision is more complex than either "soul" or "identity." In my worldview, we carve not only the ego, or the false self, but a plethora of lower selves, each fleshed out by the seed of the transient ego. Every time we misfire in our search for Self-knowledge, or aim wrong by identifying ourselves with that which is not *Atman*, we balloon the ego into existence. Each lower self is the temporary articulation of oneself ... constructed through engagement with the empirical world. Each lower self is therefore an aura of one's character, or cohort of *samskaras* (*karmic* impressions that act as dispositions) emanating from the *karmic* map one creates by engaging with the external world ... in the immanent state, prior to true Self-knowledge or *Brahma-Nirvana*.[5] Each self is therefore a milepost that points to the distance to be traversed, to reach the universal Self ... Each indicates the degree of Self-knowing accomplished. In a wise person, the self constructed in youth is likely to differ radically from the self created in mature adulthood. The latter is likely to be closer to the universal Self ... signifying progress towards Self-knowing.

Nevertheless, the lower selves have a common core ... for at the center of each rules the ubiquitous divine *Atman*. Each lower self therefore consists of *Atman* concealed in five sheaths of the unreal and the different lower selves vary by the quality of these "coverings." As per Shankaracharya, these five sheaths or "coverings of ignorance" include the "covering" of Intellect, that of Bliss, the "vital cover," the "mental cover," and the "physical cover."[6] The trail of ever evolving lower selves constitutes our centripetal pilgrimage towards the unchanging, overarching, solitary universal Self, which is the ultimate goal and central shrine of Self-knowledge. Every time we progress towards Self-knowledge, we peel off and discard a redundant lower self, replacing it by a better, more mature, or truer (albeit still lower) self. This procession and pilgrimage of lower selves is orchestrated by the hidden power of contemplation ... a ceaseless inner flow of non-discursive knowing that impinges on being. Yet, even if temporary and ultimately redundant, no virtuous lower "self" is obsolete. Each serves its

---

[5] Swami Vivekananda defines character as the sum total of *samskaras*. See Swami Budhananda, *Overcoming Anger* (Chennai: Sri Ramakrishna Math, 2009), 50-51.

[6] Swami Prabhavananda and C Isherwood, *Shankara's Crest-Jewel of Discrimination* (Hollywood: Vedanta Press, 1975), 43-67.

purpose of bequeathing progress towards Self-knowledge. Each is a faint adumbration of the solitary all ruling Self. Where "identity" is an amoral moniker bequeathed by society, the lower selves are carved by one's own *karmic* activities. Where "soul" maintains constancy of identity all the way to the afterlife, these lower selves, each pertain to a fleeting aspect of a chimerical overall immanent identity, to be debunked as unreal, in the quest for Self-knowledge.

As an artist, I drew my main *indirect* inspiration from the mystic poet and devotee of the great Goddess Kālī, Sadhak Rāmprasād Sen (ca. 1718-1775), from eighteenth century Bengal, India. I was also inspired by the mystical poetry of Bengali Nobel laureate, Rabindranath Thakur (1861-1941). In terms of direct influences, I have used both Indian and western sources. In Poem 4, "One Thousand Suns," the picture of the thousand suns rising simultaneously was inspired by Sanjaya's words in the *Bhagavadgītā*, Chapter XI, "The Vision of God in His Universal Form" – "Suppose a thousand suns should rise together into the sky: such is the glory of the Shape of Infinite God." In Poem 5, "The One as the Many," I used Bertrand Russell's highly exteriorized "correspondence theory of truth" – the notion that truth entails *correspondence* between "belief and fact," such that beliefs do not depend on minds for their truth and the fact which renders the belief true, does not involve the mind holding the belief.[7] Poem 16, "Vision of Creation" was inspired by the *Upanishads*. In Poem 26, "Bridge of Desires," the notion that earthly happiness lies in the "interval" between two desires was taken from a sermon by Swami Adiswarananda. In the same poem, the transition from the love for power to the power of love was inspired by Jimi Hendrix's words, "When the power of love overcomes the love for power, the world will know peace." In Poem 32, "Glad Stranger," I used the phrase "alone to that great Alone," inspired by Plotinus' words in *Ennead* VI. 9 (9). 11 – "escape in solitude to the solitary," commonly translated as "flight of the alone to the Alone."[8] In the same poem I drew a causal connection between anger and desire, using Swami Turiyananda's insight that anger is concentrated desire.[9] I used this same insight in Poem 33, "Anger quenched by Love," where I added the Buddha's teaching that

[7] B A W Russell, "Truth and Falsehood," in *The Problems of Philosophy* (Oxford: Oxford University Press, 1912), 202-3.

[8] *Plotinus Enneads VI. 6-9*, trans A H Armstrong (Cambridge: Harvard University Press, 1988), 344-5, note 2, 345.

[9] *Overcoming Anger*, 27.

desire arises in the mind when we depart from truth.[10] In the same poem, I used St. Augustine's notion that the redeemed human will is enchained to the divine will.[11] In Poem 39, "Bridge of Justice," I used Aristotle's basic insight that friendship exceeds justice.[12]

In these extraordinary times, we experience the common consciousness as something fragmented ... with poetry and philosophy shorn of their organic union, and therefore moorless. If aesthetics is fractured from ethics, and politics from metaphysics, then it is hardly surprising that poetry is fractured from philosophy ... at that, unequally ... with poetry leading in one sense, and philosophy, in another. Yet, far from being enemies, poetry and philosophy mutually complete one another. Therefore, they *ought* to be uttered in the same breath. Here, I draw inspiration from Swami Vivekananda (1863-1902), who dreamed of a fusion of poetry and philosophy. I regard this work as an anthology of *philosophical* poetry. It is, in the end, a song ... the *Song of the Solipsistic One.*

I thank Sri Ramakrishna, who inspired this work. I thank the artist Haridas who designed the book cover. I thank the Trustees of Prometheus Trust for accepting my work.

[10] The Buddha says, "Mistaking the false for the true, / And the true for the false, / You overlook the heart / And fill yourself with desire." See "Choices," in *Dhammapada*, trans T Byrom (Boston: Shambhala Publications Inc., 1976), 4.

[11] In Chapter 30 of "The Enchiridion" St. Augustine says, "Accordingly, he who is the servant of sin is free to sin. And hence he will not be free to do right, until, being freed from sin, he shall begin to be the servant of righteousness. And this is true liberty, for he has pleasure in the righteous deed; and it is at the same time a holy bondage, for he is obedient to the will of God." See "The Enchiridion" in *The Works of Aurelius Augustine*, ed M Dods, vol IX (Edinburgh: T & T Clark, 1892).

[12] In *Nicomachean Ethics*, Book VIII, Passage 1, Aristotle says, "... when men are friends they have no need of justice, while when they are just they need friendship as well, and the truest form of justice is thought to be a friendly quality."

Chapter One

Prelude

1

Nativity

On the immaculate conception of the Holy Mother, Sri Sarada Devi

There by the hedges,
A row of cottages, thatched and humble,
Stand still ... each home protected by
A hibiscus tree, ablaze with flowers ...
Vermillion mark of auspiciousness.

A white temple at the water's edge
Radiates Light into the corner cottage
Where the Mother prepares.

Garbing herself in fresh cloth
After her bath in the sacred river,
She enters the temple precincts,
When suddenly, waves of
Incorporeal Light pour through the
Thick masonry of the temple walls,
Seeping through brick and mortar,
Inundating all.

Engulfing her, this molten Light
Enters her sacred womb ...
She conceives.

How still she sits before the stone image,
Whose Effulgence floods Earth with
Uncontainable Joy.

Transcending the here and now,
Reaching beyond Time, Space, and Causality,
Soaring above all specious images and Matter,
Transcending the thralldom of *Maya*,

Corralling scattered thoughts into a concentrated beam of light,
Soaring from wave to higher wave of divine Consciousness,
The Mother ascends beyond body, mind, ego.
Absorbed in the Light that seeps through matter,
She loses outer consciousness.

And as the noble assembly of gods and demigods chorus their joy,
Womankind rejoices, men bow their heads in wonder,
Ten thousand galaxies shudder in bliss,
Graded hells burst asunder, releasing their redeemed inmates,
Graded heavens erupt, releasing their shining gods,
Now seeking rebirth in a festive Earth
Preparing herself for the felicitous birth of a
Divine Incarnation –
Celestial Maiden, Mother of Creation,
Goddess of Knowledge, Ruler of good and evil,
Embodiment of Truth, a Motherforce,
The power to grant salvation concealed in her fists,
Now born a Daughter in a humble cottage.

Chapter Two

The One, The Divine Name

2

At Twilight

At twilight,
The Great Orb prepares to
Cleanse Earth of brazen light ...
Night arrives,
Wrapping in its quiet mantle,
Broken glass, advertisements, shrill traffic.

A crazed cacophony of
Trillion sounds
Tumbles discordant,
Mingling, dissipating,
Vanishing in the
Growing quietude of that
Soundless Sound.

3

The Name

In the secret chamber of the mind
A cauldron of thoughts hum and whirl ...
Thrashing thoughts, concealed in a
Miasma of emotion, dark and dense.

A waft of desire infuses each thought
With its subtle burden,
Draining the mind of real joy.
How hard it quivers, this thicket of thoughts,
Trembling with desire,
Obscuring the mind's inmost Light.

Gusts of passion ...
Anger, jealousy, lust, hatred, greed ...
Disperse the trail of desires and buffet thoughts.
Unruly billows of passions and desires
Tear asunder thought from thought,
Making each ricochet against
The delicate walls of the restless mind.

When suddenly,
Riding on an empty thought,
A ray of Light appears
On the horizon of the mind,
Expressing the Divine Name.

Spreading its limitless aura,
Infusing the tranquil Name into
Every constellation of turbulent thoughts,
This illumined Thought, a harbinger of peace
Sublimates the passions, diffuses desire,
Transforming the mind,
Until every thought vibrates in unison,
Chorusing the Divine Name.

4

One Thousand Suns

As sadness grew on Earth,
A pall of gloom spread its mantle
And nation warred against nation ...
As ghettos and concentration camps
Pock-marked the hills, like ominous patches of nettle ...
As cloudbursts of bombs rained down on the valley
And lesions scarred both Earth and Man ...
As children died of malnutrition and disease
And starving mothers repelled their little ones from shrunken breasts ...
As Power raped and rampaged, turning mothers into chattel,
Demanding the birth of sons ... as women bore children in servitude ...
As the body became a badge of self, self-worth, power, hierarchy ...
As corporeal beauty, body consciousness and sheer physicality vivified materiality,
Blinding the eye, deafening the ear, coating the palate, deadening the senses ...

Something happened!

Inside the secret chambers of the psyche
Where the somatic is beheld, the body exploded –
Dismembered by the estranged Logic of Advertisement.
Thousand shadowy slivers of body parts flew asunder.
In every street corner, billboards blared aloud the body,
Degrading it, exposing it unto exhaustion,
Mutilating it for the sake of products,
Each product defining a body part, not the body the product ...
Socks defined feet, gloves defined hands,
Not the feet the socks, nor the hands the gloves.
Nobody saw the whole body.

As the carnal gaze withered the body
Into somatic relics, severing it from love and ethics,
Reducing it to a reified object –
Manufactured, distorted, produced, manicured,
Tortured and sedimented into materiality,
To provoke, entice, allure, arousing tinsel passions,

Sinking man further in the Quagmire of Delusion ...
As men plundered, ransacking Earth of her hallowed fecundity,
Nature became merchandise, with price tags on sea shells ...
And as seasons shifted unseasonably,
As animals howled in desolation and pain,
And as the waters rose and fell
Devouring some with floods, inflicting droughts on others ...
As the logic of war spread its greenish hell,
Its mushroom cloud scorching every timbre of life ...
As children played with grisly toys,
As revolutionaries repeated the wheel of violence ...

Something happened!

Silence spread its mantle ... draping wounds with healing balm,
Cradling Earth on the eternal bosom of the Divine Mother.
And as this Motherforce, a stark Power of Reality
Arose from the dark bowels of the Universe,
Spreading vitality, kindling Self-respect,
It conquered worldly power ... Its supreme caricature ...
Epitome of the unreal and parody of strength ...
Cleaving this ghostly anti-thesis into its twin halves –
Shredding the sadistic ... uprooting the masochistic.
From the ashes of this worldly power, now slain,
Rose the phoenix of Divine Love, released by
The Motherforce ... Embodiment of Truth and true Power.

And as Light continued to grow, shadows shrank ...
The dark night shriveled away, like curtains parting
On a stage awaiting a Pantomime.

For on the lone horizon
Suddenly ...

One Thousand Suns rose together
Scorching the horizon ...
There they came, rolling across the
Infinite sky, like flaming dice ...
A wondrous march of the Thousand Suns,
Igniting all with their Joyful Light.

One Thousand Suns came rolling by
Compelling a dazzling dawn,
Thundering in silence, their rumble of titanic Joy,
Transporting Earth to an Ocean of Felicity.
Gigantic Suns linked arms to embrace Earth,
Flooding all with Divine Light,
The power of Love melting all,
The power of Awe petrifying all ...
One Thousand Suns ...
Their collective Splendor too marvelous to behold!

The Silent One –
Infinite, shining Meadow
Upon whose bosom, the many meander –
The Silent One, inmost, utmost Being of each being,
That Silent One, a Motherforce,
Appeared in the form of this Solar Multitude –
The procession of the Thousand Suns.

Like dice tossed across the universe
By careless gamblers
One Thousand Suns came rolling by.

5

The One as the Many

The Divine appears as the many,
Wearing the gossamer veil of multiplicity,
Donning the diverse unreal costumes of
The range of beings It unleashes –
From the dung beetle
To the choral reef glistening in the waters –
Each guise, a quiver of multiplicity ...
For Divinity is the Absolute Ground of
All relative existence.

When, as the Great Sun, Spirit appears
Through the haze of multiplicity,
Distilling the opacity of matter,
With Its power of Reality,
It does not merely shine through matter ...
As if wholly extraneous.
For Spirit is the nucleus of opaque matter.

Spirit appears as matter,
The One appears as the many ...
Yet retains a teasing otherness.

Lacy fronds of the stately palm,
Humble willow stooping low,
Slender leaves blowing in the wind,
Mountain paths winding down the hill,
Rooftops thundering with monsoon rain,
Undulating hills clad in snow,
Endless steppes shimmering with dew,
Ten thousand petals showering upon
The dark serenity of an unsuspecting night –
All this is Divine.

The Truthforce of Science, its beauty,
Its homage to proportion, logic and the laws of nature,
Its springboard of the Correspondence notion of Truth ...
The power of this Truth to pierce through bias,
With a ruthless objectivity that shatters sentimentality –
All this is Divine.

The beauty of poetic inspiration and ideas,
The harmony of all cadres of truth –
From the scientific to the poetic –
All this is Divine.

The supernal beauty of virtue –
A mother's love, a father's love, the love of an animal ...
The supernal beauty of Compassion –
Objective, wise, undistracted by spectacles of pain ...
The supernal beauty of filaments of detached Love
That string the universe into a
Seamless Whole, vibrating with empathy ...
The supernal beauty of the invisible warmth
That enshrouds each suffering being –
All this is Divine.

Even man made things –
Refrigerator, Bookshelf, Computer
Automobile, Copy Machine, Hubble Telescope –
All marvels of technology, modern or ancient,
All these are Divine too.
For bereft of their Divine Substratum, they are nihil.

Neither good, nor evil, nor a mere knowing of Truth,
The Divine is Truth Itself ...
Truth that towers beyond good and evil,
Truth unalloyed by valuation.
The Divine is the Existential Ground of
The Good and the Beautiful –
But also the Shining Substratum of evil.

Upon the endless Meadow of the Divine
Evil churns, kindling wicked waves of
The irrational, the demonic – both man made and natural.

When the tsunami ... unwilled, menacing ...
Devours innocent millions – this too is Divine.
When vitriolic earthquakes lick whole townships –
This too is Divine.
When droughts and famines extinguish innocent lives –
This too is Divine.

Nature echoes seismic tremors of human thoughts ...
Translating these tangible, willed

Reverberations of the common consciousness
To unwilled natural phenomena.
When the inexorable hand of mechanical Nature
Smites without malice – this too is Divine.

All mindless cruelty, every vice that proliferates
Chilling chambers of mental isolation,
Inflating the ego, decimating Self-respect –
All this is laced with the Divine –
The one and only Real Substratum
That laces every unreal hell.

For the greatest act of malevolence caused by man or Nature,
Cannot occur, unless permitted by God –
Being Absolute, Knowledge Absolute, Bliss Absolute.

For good and evil are one among
Countless pairs of opposites that buzz like bees,
Whirling in the unreal world of derived, relative existence.
When the Divine casts Its benevolent eye upon good and evil
It sees two sides of the same coin.

Yet, for the unenlightened,
There is one means only of surmounting sin –
To actualize and express the divine potential buried deep within –
To awaken from a consciousness sullied by sin
To the Divine as Pure Consciousness.

How?

By letting ...
Good overcome evil,
Merit overcome demerit.

Good is valuable, not in itself, but in its unique power of Expiation –
Good can purify evil. Good can vanquish evil.
Neither good nor evil are solid substances.
If good can erase evil, then evil can erase good.
Yet good and evil are not symmetrical twins.
Good is far stronger, more concentrated than evil.
For the power of goodness to expiate evil ...
This is real power ... or the power of divine Reality, whereas
Evil's power to destroy good is a chimerical flame of worldly power,
Rooted in the abyss of the unreal.

The Divine Spectator towers so high, yet
Pervades each being, as its Shining Substratum.
Neither good nor evil, but a silent witness,
This Spectator regards both with equanimity –
With the equal, just eye of Divine Love.

Far away, by the laughing brook,
In a solitary hut lives the solitary Sage.
Adorned with Omnivision, she is clairvoyant ...
She can see the Divine in the greatest evil –
Not as extraneous Light infusing its Omnipresence –
An Omnipresence that enters a separate entity ...
Like the color that trickles across a canvas,
Like the light that hastens to scatter darkness,
Like the good that rushes to dispel evil –
But as that which is beyond good and evil –
As the supra-moral Infinitude,
That towers beyond all opposites ...
And yet remains ubiquitous –
For this Reality is both transcendent and immanent.

Omniscient visionary ... the Sage can see
The Divine Substratum, lying still
Beneath the chimerical pairs of opposites,
Letting light, darkness, and all the pairs
Flicker across the Canvas of the Divine
Like unreal shadows playing upon the
Infinite meadows of the solitary Real.

This ancient Sage can see the Divine Substratum,
Concealed ... quiescent ... yet, shining through the
Unreal shadows of good and evil that
Flicker across Its iridescent Countenance.

6

Language, a Divine Ladder

From the empty froth of words,
Churning in an ocean of sounds,
Bereft of reason –
Language is born.

From a storm of words,
Meandering in stochastic ways,
Threatening to descend to
The Abyss of a sooty imagination,
Torn asunder from the inborn mantic flames
That bind together the soul of speech –
Language is born.

What is Grammar –
But a torchlight of reason, a skeleton of Language,
A shepherd of words, a Grid of Truth and
Divine vessel, brimming with latent words,
Spilling forth its pure lexical light –
A light that transforms the foaming dithyramb of words,
Spiraling in an inky abyss – into beautiful logical threads that
Infuse meaning, drawing music from the chatter of blind wordshells.

When all far flung words are
Corralled into shapes by Grammar –
Language is born.

When an ocean of words is strung in logical threads
That garland the Pure Light of the One –
Language is born.

The morning Sun spreads its fingers of light,
Repelling the dark night ...
When like the Sun, this first light of reason
Launches on its maiden flight,
It begets a chorus of radiant reason
From the light of Language –
With the reason in grammar attuned to

The reason in the meaning of words
And the reason in the sounds of words.

Under the ambiance of this trinitarian melody of reason
Words are transformed to the subtle, the poetic ...
Words are transported to the magnet of the mantic
Embedded in the shining *telos* of Language.

But the Light of the One still shines afar – unreachable ...
For the speaker lingers in the outer portals,
Mesmerized by the hypnotic beauty of wordshells,
As if mistaking fireflies for stars.

What are these husks of true Light that enchant the speaker?
Wordshells – words that stand statuesque
Outside the portals of the inmost shrine ...
Barren words – elegant in form and sound, but blind –
Unaware of the Terrific Radiance flooding the worlds
From the inmost bowels of the unshakable One.

And though the speaker ascends
From grammar to words, from words to thoughts
Each step more subtle ...
How enmeshed she remains in the Cosmic Illusion ...
Enchanted by the unreal ocean of Language.
Mindless of her luminous destination, she is
Unaware that she is in love with mere wordshells ...
Oysters that contain the pearl of Language –
A pearl that enfolds unending waves of Pure Light!

Through the poetry conjured by the chorus of
A subtle grammar, subtler words, still subtler thoughts,
One revealing the next,
Language is a radiant ladder exploding with
The turgid power of words, transporting the soul –
From mortality to immortality, from clamor to silence,
From darkness to Light, from chaos to poetry,
From the twin signs of inner destitution –
Lexical opulence and lexical famine –
From the extreme winds of both to
The profound silence of the Divine Name.

For although mantic, this Lexical Ladder
Is a shining corpse until the Light above
Touches the crest of each word wave
With the Divine Name,
Casting a sheen of gold upon the ocean of words,
Enlivening it, imbuing it with Truth,
Enabling this unending unreal ocean to disclose
The hallowed Being of beings now concealed as
The Solitary Substratum that supports this ocean.

And as Language comes alive, throbbing with strength,
Shining with borrowed Light, it ascends higher,
Replacing each sound with its matching slot of silence.
As silence grows, and being unfolds, and the ocean is wrung dry,
This lexical sea shrivels to that succinct treasure trove –
A cryptic rosary of words aglow with mantic power –
Mantras that utter the hallowed Divine Name.

From an ocean of words ...
From the chatter of thoughts ...
From clamor and confusion ... to the magnetic silence cast by
The iridescent *Mantric* words that ferry the Divine Name.

And as silence deepens, even those few words vanish
Like footprints in virgin snow.
Every sound in the cosmos melts to its universal Root ...
A Root that chimes ceaselessly, silently
That eternal primordial sound – *"Aum"* ...
We reach the Divine as Original Sound,
When every minor sound in the universe ...
From the softest whisper to the loudest roar ...
Is distilled to the Soundless Sound that
Vibrates across the created worlds,
Comforting all, sustaining all, animating all.

Eternal Ancestor,
Creative source of all sound,
Perpetual Hum, Ambrosial Chime,
Celestial Root –
"Aum" devours every Language.

Divine Gardener

The mind was an unkempt landfill,
Choking with thought weeds,
Blowing with winds of passion
That scattered thought seeds,
Festering with thought nettles and brambles,
Quaking with tangled thought roots that
Burrowed deep into the fetid soil of the mind.

And as warring thoughts wrestled one another
For dominion over the mind ... as strife descended into chaos,
And good thoughts succumbed to the twin toxins of anger and hatred ...
As the mind disintegrated, tumbling down an inky vortex,
Spiraling away from reason ...
The Divine Gardner arrived with the sure stealth of Time.

Infusing the first dewdrop of Pure Love
Into a mind churning with anger,
The Gardener let this powerful Love spread its halo –
A palliative tincture, Love spread in ever widening rings,
Diffusing anger, vanquishing hatred.
Like a distant star shining upon the moon,
Pure Love ruled the thralldom of reason.

The Divine Gardener let this droplet of Love
Seep into the soil of the mind, refreshing thought roots
Tossing out thought weeds, planting fresh thought flowers
And thought trees laden with luscious fruits of thought virtues.

And as the Gardener converted the landfill of the mind
Into a garden blooming with thought flowers,
Their fresh scents filling the sweet air of the mind,
A thought mist spraying virtue across every flowerbed,
The Divine Name arrived, riding on a luminous thought throne.

And as the Name cast its glorious glance
Upon the garden of scintillating thoughts, shimmering with virtues,

Discrete thoughts separated, like tones in a melody.
The Divine Name pierced each thought, lifting it beyond good and evil,
Filling it with molten Light that oozed forth
Through the porous walls of each blossoming thought,
Until the mind became a shining mass of purified thoughts –
Turgid with liquid Light ...

The Name gave birth to the nascent Word,
And as the Word hurtled out of the Name,
It tore down every thought wall,
Swollen with the plenitude of excess Light ...
It bound this shining mass of thoughts together,
Wringing them clean of Language,
Stilling this haze of Light that is Language
Until it ceased to be.

Now the Word returned to its origin
In the Womb of the Name
And the Mind Garden vanished
In the trail of extinguished thoughts ...
These disappeared because they coalesced
Into a silent shining mass of blinding beads of
Pure incorporeal Light,
Vibrating with the Divine Name.

8

Sunset and Joy

Sunset and blushing Sky,
Fading blue, crimson lined,
Crescent Moon, shining sickle,
Distant Star, speck of Love,
And amidst these matchless cosmic minstrels
Chiming the same hymn –
One puff of cotton wool Cloud
Floating with nonchalance ... an afterthought,
The last brush-stroke of the Master Painter –
The all knowing One who paints upon Himself ...
For He is the Canvas, the Color, and all that He colors.

Serene Sky bathes this graceful Earth in hallowed silence,
As the teeming throng of Gods and Demigods
Begin their choral hymn of silent adoration.
Sky ripples with their melodious tones,
As the Music of Joy vibrates across Creation
And Delight descends from the
Discerning bowels of the Silent One, in quiet laps,
Like waves murmuring on a shoreline.

With holy Charity Joy fuses the many into One,
Both within and without ...
Joy integrates the flock of meandering thoughts
Into the steadfast Hum of the unuttered One.
And in the external world of quivering multiplicity,
Joy fuses the many in holy Charity ...
Like a good shepherd, Joy steers all stragglers
Into the same Divine One, seemingly outside our minds.

Joy betroths each being to the all Holy One
Putting each in a state of hallowed suspension and inebriation,
Leaving each being detached and gliding through the storm of life,
A compassionate Spectator –
Neither touching, nor caught in the trap of cloying attachment.

And as the setting sun turns a page in the Book of Time,
As the dying Day ushers the inky Night,
All valuation ceases –
For we ascend in the hymnal silence of self-transcendence,
Beyond the thralldom of good and evil ...
We join the hallowed procession of Contemplation
Returning to the radiance of the Unuttered One.

Sunset and enchanting Sky ...
Every Divine brushstroke upon the Great Painting
Vanishes in the thrill of Cosmic Union,
Vibrating with Eternal Joy,
As the Master Painter erases His Painting
With one stroke of Pure Joy,
Gathering His meandering flock back to Himself ...
Gathering them back from the mirage of multiplicity,
He leaves behind nothing but Himself ...
That forceful Reality – the one and only One!

9

Hermit in the Sun

Enthroned in the central shrine of the sky,
The Great Sun radiates Its gift of Light,
Inundating the sky with the free flood of Joy.

Inexhaustible Fountain,
The Great Sun overflows with endless warmth, power, Love
Washing with undying Light every secret crevice in consciousness,
Nourishing the teeming foliage that craves alms from the Sun.

Inexhaustible Lantern,
The Great Sun warms the tear drop like oceans whose
Lapping waves also crave alms from our Solar Star.

Mankind recognizes this Star as
The roaring Fire of Reality, exuding
Flames of Contemplation that
Elicit from men the procession of virtues
Led by two monarchs – Renunciation and Self-surrender.

From deep within the great Coiling Sun
Whirling with the might of Contemplation,
Flames leap forth to project the mirage of the created worlds.
Yet the mirage and its holy Solar Substrate are strung in a mutual bond –
The Great Sun, which creates the created worlds, is in turn, created by
these worlds.
Inspired by the Sun, the holiest of human thoughts waft upwards,
From the mirage that is Earth ...
Thoughts made buoyant by the magnetic pull of the Sun ...
But held aloft by the power of their lofty contents.
Yet the Sun, in turn draws power by inhaling these holy thoughts ...
How furiously It coils, animated by the kinetic force of these thoughts.

Buffeted by solar winds, fueled by holy human thought ...
Yet the Great Sun is calm ... utterly still,
Its centripetal pull balanced by its centrifugal push.

A fiery whirlpool, coiling quietly within Itself
In repeated motions of Contemplation –
This whirling Rosary, the outer rim
Leads to the serene center of the Sun.

On this auspicious day,
Fecund with the promise of Grace,
Mankind looks fearlessly at the blazing Sun,
Its eyes unfazed, its thoughts athirst
For the Light of the Sun.

What does it see in the central shrine,
Where solar winds have died,
Devoured by the calming centripetal pull
From the Center of the Sun ...
What does it see but
The Great God of Renunciation ...

As this unmoved, ashen, luminous Hermit
Sits still in the blazing shrine of the Sun,
He radiates the roaring flames of the Sun's
Fire of Contemplation ... flames that emanate from
The depths of Shiva's absorption in meditation.
For contemplation is the centrifugal aura of meditation.

A silent Hermit sits still, surrounded by
Flames that coil with the mute power of contemplation –
Flames that serve as His halo,
But also as the disciples that rush to Him.

Shiva –
Rapt in meditation, His throat blue,
Poisoned by human thought toxins
He has redeemed effortlessly
By His act of Grace ...

Shiva –
Redeems the children of Earth,
His white body smeared with
Gray ashes of renunciation,
His meditating eyes turned inwards

Beholding and entering in supreme silence
The luminous space of
The innards of the created worlds
Which lie within Him.

Shiva –
A beautiful fountain of baptismal water
Flows from His disheveled locks,
Every wave of this Holy River
An aqueous aura of His Divine Thoughts,
An aqueous form of His Divine Breath.
Devouring the eternal strife between
Fire and Water, this blessed fountain of
The purifying Essence of Water finds amity
With the blazing Fire of Contemplation.

Shiva –
A Divine Fountain, is also a Divine Magnet –
He exerts a push and a pull.
Despite the flames,
A Holy River springs out of His matted locks
Befriending the Fire of Contemplation.

10

There is a Radiant Womb

There is an illumined Womb –
Beyond the throbbing galaxies,
Beyond the noble constellations,
Beyond the graded heavens,
Beyond the graded hells,
Beyond this beautiful Earth
And the miasma of
Time, Space, Becoming, Death.

And yet ...
That which is beyond, is also within ...
This Womb which is beyond also shines forth from
Deep within the miasma, in a twofold manner ...
Circling and enfolding each being, on the outside,
It cocoons the immanent with Its own sublime Immanence.
But this Womb also shines forth from within each being ...
Whether sentient or not.
For each being is an immanent lamp,
Shining with the inner Light of this Luminous Seed,
Being Absolute, and Holy Substrate.

There is a blessed Womb –
That transcends mind and body,
A storehouse of holy thoughts
That belong to everybody, because they belong to nobody.
For the greatest thoughts are divine gifts,
Dispensed freely as vehicles of
Holy wisdom, self-control and the glowing retinue of virtues
That adorn the soul, like fresh foliage adorns the tree.

There is a radiant Womb –
Origin of Truth, beyond good and evil,
Origin of Creation, Source of Grace,
Cause of Enlightenment, Abode of the Enlightened,
A Providential Home that uplifts all who have lost hope ...

Comforts all who are buried in despair and dread ...
Cradles all who double over, mute with pain
In grimy torture cells ...

There is a shining Womb –
Overflowing with Light,
Infusing healing tinctures of Divine Aspiration
In souls that struggle to shed self-darkening weights of
Desire and sin that tug away at their flesh ...
A Womb that imbues souls with
The radiant wings of Dispassion and Discrimination –
Wings that carry them back from their sojourn in the unreal,
To the Reality that is this Womb.

There is an auspicious Womb –
That ensconces all Creation ...
Promising deliverance from body and mind
For this Reality reaches beyond
The thought tortured thralldom of mind.

Why is this Womb Transcendent?
Because It is Immanent ...
Why is It Immanent?
Because It is Transcendent ...

Chapter Three

Cosmic Union, Cosmology, Cosmic Illusion, Afterlife

11

Two Suns

The mind was an ocean
Caught between two horizons.

Irascible, restless with desire,
The mind churned towards
The false horizon, where
The glittering sun of desire,
A grand illusion, reigned supreme –
Tempting, beguiling, emitting rays of
Serpentine desires that evoked
Seismic thought waves in a
Flamboyant forgery of Light ...

There they flow like moths to their pyre,
Waves of desire seeking futile repose –
In the futility of a distant shoreline
That does not exist –
In a mirage that causes the mind to
Keel over from its noble Pedestal of Truth.

Suddenly the flow ceases
As the sober radiance of Grace
Seizes the waves,
Revolving them imperceptibly.
As if the current has changed,
The waves now face the Other Horizon.

And as they thirst for the calm repose of a
Real shoreline, these waves are blinded –
Before them rises the Sun of Reality ...
An Emperor, flinging magnificent rays
Upon all and sundry,
Illumining all the worlds, debunking the sun of desire,
Revealing this grand illusion for what it is.

And as the royal Sun of Reality
Rises higher and higher,
Ruling the sky supreme
Emitting ferocious golden rays,
Its reflections trembling upon
The waters of the mind,
Illumining the foam crested crown of
Each swarthy thought wave,
Casting a sheen of pure gold upon
The quivering waters of the mind,
As all this glory unfolds ...
Falsity fades before Blinding Reality.

And as the phantom sun of desire
Wilts in the heat of the Sun of Reality,
The mind sees a marvelous sight –
Two discs in motion,
One Titanic Sun rising, as the other fades.
And with every upward surge
This flaming Surge of Reality
Devours in large bites the phantom sun
Which fades like the morning mist.
As the Sun of Reality rises in pulsating laps,
As if breathing ... as if brightening with each breath,
Its ghostly other, the tinsel sun of desire
Disappears on the opposite shore.

And as the Sun of Reality rises higher and higher
The waves of the mind roll rhythmically –
Drawn by this Divine Magnet.

Shedding dross and desires, renouncing
The Black Hole of the Cosmic Illusion
In the mirage-like shoreline,
Now bereft of its phantom sun,
These thought pilgrims
Ascend the steep slope of the Divine Disc,
Climbing this invisible Mountain of Truth,
A shining citadel of Pure Consciousness that
Radiates the calm ambiance of sheer Reality.

12

Living Flames

The universe is ensconced in a
Boundless Womb of Light ...
A mystical Womb that contains the universe,
Yet pervades it, for
This Divine Substratum of all that becomes ...
Is both Macrocosm and Microcosm.

The universe is enshrouded by
A Fire that shines with infinite Power ...
Infinite in Its every infinite dimension –
Beyond language, beyond number
Beyond the created worlds that
Cascade from Its Living Flames.

Seemingly far from this blinding Light,
In a corporeal universe humming with
Glorious orbs, festive constellations, brilliant stars,
Perhaps the most humble of these whirling tops,
Why, a renunciate ... is Earth.

Yet dwelling on this planet of no obvious consequence
Is the finite human mind ... a universe unto itself
Where thoughts hum and whirl,
Moved by the winds of passions and desires.
Like the heavenly bodies meandering in the endless cosmos,
Embodied thoughts vibrate and wander in the cosmos of the mind.

Although a mundane planet, bereft of glamour,
Earth cannot be innocuous.
Although a speck of dust on Earth,
Which is a speck of dust in the crowded cosmos,
Man cannot be innocuous ...
For, inside his mind You hide!

Existence Absolute and Master of *Maya*,
You hide within every being ... sentient, insentient,
In all the created worlds.
For You are the Substratum of all relative existence.

And when we cast aside the distorting prism of relativity,
The universe itself is revealed to be nothing but You,
As are all the created worlds ...
The myriad heavens, hells ... all their dwellers.
For in the end You alone exist ...
You are draped in unreal shadows ...
These cobwebs being
The limiting adjuncts of names and forms.

But once you sound your Bugle,
Declaring your Name, thoughts drift no further.
They begin their immortal dance –
A pilgrimage from the finite to the Infinite.

This conflagration of the Divine Name,
Makes drifting thoughts catch fire from
The Blazing Infinitude ... both within and without.
For this Boundless Fire pervades as the Microcosm, or
Flaming Indwelling Seed ... Nucleus of each porous thought.
But as the Macrocosm, this Fire "ensconces" the universe.

When suddenly,
One thought breaks free, flying beyond
The choppy sea of turbulent thoughts –
Beyond mind and its awareness of body.
And as this thought ascends to the crest of
Pure Consciousness, the mind loses
Awareness of the sensory world.

As the Divine Fire ensconcing the universe
Now reveals Its full glory through the medium of
The Name swathed in the shell of a single thought,
All external body consciousness is lost.

And what does the mind see as it rises
Beyond body, thought, ego,
Molting skeins of mind parts,
Ascending to the substratum of
Pure Consciousness?

It sees ...

Living Flames, Light immortal,
Glowing embers of Divine Infinitude,
Ocean of Fire ...
Knowledge Absolute, Being Absolute, Bliss Absolute.

13

The Universe and Beyond

This universe is a compound of limitless space ...
Yet confined by the amity of materiality with multiplicity,
Each stolen from its corresponding twin,
Flying helter skelter amidst the pairs of opposites
That buzz like bewildered bees in the created worlds ...
The opposites are divine instruments that conjure
The chimera of the star studded cosmos.

And as the Sage meditates on –
The One that conjures this Cosmic Illusion,
The One that bears the mirage of multiplicity,
The One so rapt in Its Divine Sport,
The One that is a Sole Reality –
She flies through the window into the fresh night air.
Sweet scents of blossoms perfume this air
As she glides over the gentle undulation of hill and dale,
Rising past mountain tops, catapulting into the firmament above,
Sweeping past the garland of planets surrounding the ferocious Sun
Glowering in the central shrine of the solar system.

She peers into the festive, ornate galaxies
Alive and churning, exploding with lights,
Festooned like ancient lanterns,
Exulting in the Divine Name ...
A merciless Name that expunges all cesspools of darkness,
Peeling off dross, melting hardened stalactites of Sin.

The stars skip and dance ...
The Sage is caught in this stellar dance,
Caught between light and shade,
Caught between Matter and Space,
Caught between torrid gusts of multiplicity.

When suddenly, the curtains part ...

They reveal
A divine rainshower of incorporeal Light,
A cool, soothing downpour that devours

The dream world of multiplicity,
Leaving the Sage bereft of awareness of body and mind.

And as she transcends the material universe,
Rising through the subtle universe,
Flying past shining galaxies of gods and demigods,
Into that alcove of Divine Ideas,
Ensconced in an Ocean of Light,
Suddenly the universes ... both material and subtle
Burst like a pair of bubbles ...
They vanish, leaving behind the one and only Reality ...
Unbounded Ocean of Ambrosial Light.

In this spaceless Light, the Sage swims
Until she becomes a glowing Flame
Transmuted to a ray of Light
That mingles with the calm sea of
Infinite, endless Light.

14

Joy to the Hells

Joy to the world!
Joy to the heavens!
And a special, nameless Joy,
Distilled by the heavens, to the
The slow unwinding caravan of
Smoldering graded hells,
Traversing the miasma of Becoming ...
For the graded heavens, lodged also
In this moving mirage of Becoming
Are luminous Spectators,
Like quiet city lights shining
Upon distant hills.
Yet they are not aloof ...
They do not watch idly, as the hells smolder ...
For each shining heaven adopts a dreary hell
Absolving it with its native stock of Divine Joy.

Each whirling hell smolders with
Wrath, acrimony, hatred
As its bemused inmates expiate their sins,
Shedding weight by obeying painstakingly
The golden logic of the God given, invisible
Karmic Ledger, that tots up merit and demerit
Over the span of a Dynamic Judgment Day.

This solitary dynamic Cosmic Day ...
Equal in length to limitless Time ...
Unwinds across the fleeting infinitude of Time ...
It rules the plethora of the Created Worlds.

When gusts of salubrious Joy
Rush out of the heavens
Into the moth eaten innards of
Grimy, multi-tiered hell-dungeons –
They stall their labor,

They stall their expiatory mills
Which begin to unwind like tired windmills ...
When the supreme salubrious sunlight of Joy
Arrives to thaw in an instant
Every stalactite of sin ...
When Joy expiates, Joy unshackles, and
Joy bursts opens the mammoth smoking doors of
Multiple seething hells ... when Joy rushes in,
Ventilating these dithyrambic hells,
Refreshing each with the fragrance of virtue ...
Then, like a swarm of butterflies set free by
The onset of spring that replenishes Earth,
The once wild inmates, laboring to shower themselves
At the grinding mills of expiation,
Rush out, in the delirious Joy of Moral Freedom ...

A strange freedom indeed ...

For this supernal liberty wrought by morality,
Is the same freedom that frees *from* morality –
As good expiates evil unto
A full transcendence of good and evil.

As Joy baptizes, washing clean
Every nook and cranny of each dreary hell,
Expunging all musty cobwebs of sin,
The created worlds halt their grinding daily chores.
They halt so they can Listen ...

Everything hushes, everything halts
As each listens to the Music of the Spheres ...
To the Choral Music of Divine Inebriation
Vibrating through quivering ranks of multiplicity ...

And what do they see
As they listen thus?

They see a shining ocean of graceful gyrations,
Rhyming with the celestial cadences of this Divine Music ...
They see enchanting movements of Joy
In a dancing Cosmos where

Every orb orbits in the exuberance of Joy,
As all rejoice to celebrate the long procession of
Prodigal sons and daughters returning home,
Flying free from the landscape of hells,
Now released and absolved of every sin
By the supreme Power of Divine Joy
Emanating from the One and only One –
Through the tiered constellation of glowing Heavens.

Now, upon contemplating the Power of the One,
They understand that all heavens, hells, every bit of Creation –
All are parts of the Cosmic Illusion ...
All fall within the supreme Mirage
Conjured by the Conjurer upon His own bosom.
For He is the only Reality ...

What are good, evil, heaven, hell?
What is moral valuation?
No more than actors in the Cosmic Illusion –
Ghosts in a ghostly world.

Like our supreme, paradigmatic Actor-Spectator ... the One,
Each thinking being is a joyful actor-Spectator –
An actor in the ghostly mirage, a Divine Spectator in potentiality –
A Spectator actualized upon journeying from hell to heaven and beyond,
An actor-pilgrim that converts to Spectator, when she casts aside
The mirage of multiplicity to become rooted in the
Divine roost of our one and only Reality.

15

The Invisible

Man, who longs to create –
To express his essence in an external creation,
Connected, yet severed from his existence,
Thus prolonging his mortality beyond Death,
By lingering in human memory through his creation
After his mortal frame dies –
This man, despite all his gifts, cannot create Life ...

This wise constraint upon his God given faculties
Frustrates man enough that he rips through all boundaries,
Like a mighty river breaking all bounds,
Flooding its shores in delirious anger.

Man who loses his way in the wilderness of worldliness
Because he has forgotten his God given solitary vocation of
Self realization, this forlorn man – so alone in the universe
And blinded by his lack of Self-knowledge –
Creates with fury, multiplying his needs, flooding the world
With a glut of titillating, soul deadening products ...

The weary soul is torn asunder, cleft apart,
Bruised and maimed, by the twisted arrows of
Its crazed cleaving to things, things, and still more things –
Visible, insentient products that leave behind
Their fatal footprints on the fading soul
Burdening its diluted gaze.

When suddenly, its ghost is seized, its Light returns,
For it has been touched by the Invisible ...

Through the silky night Sky
Dotted by a storm of stars ...
Through this translucent Firmament
Midnight blue and throbbing with Love,
Shines the Invisible ...

Stars upon stars, a fountain of stars,
Stars that glisten like grains of sand,
Stars that revolve round and round
Whirling with the power of Contemplation,
Glowing forever in the subtle fervor of Prayer,
Drawing their power from the magic spell,
Cast upon them by their Fountainhead,
The Invisible, which infuses Life into their
Modest stellar light, *bewitching* them ...

This storm of stars heals forever
Our worldly world, draining it of all
Opiating worldliness.

Against the comforting space of that Night Sky
Quivering with multiplicity,
There flies a flock of snow white geese,
Their wings bewitched by the
Stealthy touch of stellar light.

The soul once stung by the thousand nettles of
A thousand possessions, now casts them off
Like a tree shedding leaves when autumn commands.
This trembling soul, free at last of finite things,
Yet still confined in the prison of finitude,
This enchained soul now escapes finitude
By dissolving itself within Infinitude –

The Invisible!

16

Vision of Creation

Immersed in the Ocean of Pure Consciousness,
The Sage saw, bobbing in and out –
Appearing and disappearing,
Like blocks of ice riding the sea waves,
Innumerable luminous Cosmic Eggs –
Elliptical solar systems, shining joyfully,
Each with its ornate ruling god,
Each with its assembly of demigods,
Bobbing in and out, riding the waves of
Eternal Consciousness –
All this upon the Cosmic Body of
The one and only One.

17

Thought-Mirrors

The mind was a meadow
Planted with upturned, circular mirrors –
Each gleaming disc, a thought illumined by
The Fiery Orb that radiates all-powerful beams of Light
Upon the sky of the mind.

Catching the conflagration of
This life giving Light,
Each thought-mirror begins to
Shine with borrowed Light –
Shedding all dross, expanding,
Turning into a shining, spherical
Crystal of sheer Light.

Each thought-crystal swells
Until it bursts into subtle thought-mists.

Shining mist-like billows of Light mingle with
Shining mist-like billows of Grace
Leaving behind footprints –
Shining beads of unalloyed Joy.

18

Majestic Solitude

At first, quivering waves of multiplicity –
Difference, difference everywhere ...

The maple, the oak, the elm
The banana, the banyan, the palm,
Every leaf different, every flower different, every hue different.
The air teems with a kaleidoscope of multiplicity –
August assembly of gods and demigods,
Boisterous throngs that crowd the market square of life ...
Men, women, children, herds of impassioned animals,
Racing wraiths that move like the wind.
The air teems with a kaleidoscope of multiplicity –
The roar of the mountain lion, the vigil of the lonely leopard,
The sky crackling with thunderous winds of multiplicity
That churn the heavens.

Difference, difference everywhere ...

Whirling orbs orbiting,
Constellations of stars – festive, secretive,
They harbor dark whirlpools in their midst ...
The silent chatter of heavenly bodies
Add to the obscuring cloud of unknowing.

When suddenly Light seeps in from every direction ...
Pouring in through the porous walls of the permeable mind,
Through the frail walls of each fragile thought and
Through the cardboard heavens –
Drowning the universe in sheer radiance,
Dissolving all sounds in the grand Infinitude and
Eternal peal of the Divine Ambrosial Hum.

Blinding invisible Light,
Deafening, silent Sound
Both hammer away, obliterating differences,

Compelling amity –
As if ... merely as if ... synthesizing thoughts,
Congealing life-forms, integrating multiplicity.

But this is only seeming ...
For the Light and Sound unify
Not by integrating multiplicity ...
But by awakening each being ...
To reveal its common essence.
Unity lies in the *common* One ...
Not in the summation of
The many to a *composite* one.
Where there are no differences,
Where the chimerical many *is* a shining One,
Integration is redundant!

Awakening "integrates"!
Divine Light and Sound "integrate"
By revealing discrete differences to be
Part of the Cosmic Illusion.
They "integrate"
By awakening each discrete being
To reveal the common nucleus of
The Solipsistic One that dispels all difference!

Divine Light and Sound
Awaken the potential divinity of
The contemplator rapt in meditation!
And as the "awakened" One
Recognizes the dream for a dream,
The mirage of multiplicity vanishes,
Dispelling the ephemeral universe and
The ghostly mind.

Multiplicity cannot be integrated,
For multiplicity *is* the Cosmic Illusion.
For nothing exists besides the One
Rejoicing Alone in Majestic Solitude.

19

Thought Lanterns

At first, the mind was a thoroughfare, with
Ever milling thought pedestrians trampling
The raucous marketsquare of the mind.
Its concentration scattered ...
With thought clusters focusing this way and that
In self dissipating idleness ... the mind weakened before
The scintillating scents from the worldly world
Tugging frenetically at each thought cluster ...
The mind's oceanic desires left each thought cluster
At the mercy of the clamorous world of sense objects.

Yet behind this cacophony reposes the silent eternal Spectator ...
Standing at the altar of the mind, this luminous Witness
Watches the mind dilute itself in suicidal outpourings,
Hemorrhaging its strength
As it cleaves in terror to external stimuli.

For every attachment it forms to
The ringing worldliness of the world
The mind gouges out a portion of itself,
Leaving in exchange, an empty black hole,
As if each attachment bit off a piece of the dwindling mind.

When suddenly,
All thought pedestrians cease their chatter
For a Light appears on the horizon of the mind ...
Each thought halts with bated breath,
For an enormous dazzling Thought Sun
Rises upon the boundless firmament of the mind-sky,
Splashing its Light across this canvas,
Pouring forth its warmth and heat ... relentlessly.

The mind now stalls –
Its petrified thoughts stand still,
Mesmerized by the wondrous sight of

This gigantic Sun rising higher and higher,
Its heat devouring every thought toxin,
When suddenly, they find
They can bear this Light no longer ...
Thoughts fly helter skelter
Before the might of this terrifying Sun,
Every foul thought wilting and withering,
Making room for fresh thoughts
That emanate from the Thought Sun ...
Each animated by virtue.

The Giant Thought Sun
Probes into Its offspring –
Using a flame borrowed from Itself
To kindle the inner Light of each thought
Converting each to a *virtuous* thought,
Hauling each righteous thought to
The shining pinnacle beyond good and evil.
Every thought, now a shining lantern
Inlaid with the eternal essential
Flame of the Divine Name
Transforms the mind to a festive chamber
Illumined by a carnival of gleaming
Thought Lanterns.

20

Sonic One

She listened hard to the whispering trees,
The gentle breeze, the dulcet tones of
Chirruping birds – she listened in vain.

She listened hard to the fretful waves,
The roaring storm, the menacing rumble of
The rolling thunder – she listened in vain.

She listened hard to the dissembling tones of
The thousand Octaves that hurtled down
Like autumn leaves, from the silent Heavens –
She listened in vain.

For her soul was athirst, not for creaturely sounds
But for the Divine Hum ... the Song of the *Logos*,
The Song that was the Singer Itself ... the Sonic One,
With no cleft separating Singer from Song.

For her soul was athirst
For the Song that *was* the Sonic One,
Veiled in Its own dilution of sonic multiplicity,
Veiled in the numberless sounds
Ringing through the ghostly Cosmos.

She listened in vain ...

But once the radiant One
Revealed itself to her thirsty soul,
Through the sheer medley of
Symphony and cacophony
She could wait no more ...

Now seizing a humble Chord,
Lying low in the cosmic sanctorum of spectral music,
She rode bestride this chariot of melody,
Renouncing with discernment

The million sounds that form the beguiling music of the many,
A music that veils the One and enchants the listener,
Lulling her into a metaphysical sleep of ignorance.

And as her charioteer Chord
Flew through the created worlds,
Rising higher and higher in the order of awareness,
She found the strength to resist the music of the many
For the discerning One empowered her to
Penetrate each tone, distilling each, until
She pierced through the veil of the sonic many
Reaching her repose within the
Heart of the Sonic One.

Free at last, and flinging off the flying Chord
Now ephemeral, its sound mundane,
The Sage reposes in the ultimate peace of
The Divine Hum of the Great *Logos* ...
Pristine, original Simple Song
Bereft of and prior to all clefts of otherness.

21

Rebirth

Last night she died in her sleep.
Orange Flames leapt upon her funeral pyre,
Flames of Contemplation that tried to lick clean
Every stain upon her soul,
Every fervent, ego driven desire.

Last night she was reborn
For her soul, though cleansed,
Failed to leap forth from
The Funereal Flames of Contemplation
To return to their origin –
The solitary Fire of the Great Sun, that
Flaming Source of all that is fresh and living.

Last night, she was reborn
When the last flame of Contemplation
Whimpered away, leaving behind
Lingering strains of desire that hung in her soul, like
Stubborn foliage refusing the command of Autumn.

Last night she was reborn when
The glowing phoenix of Aspiration
Flew out of the ashes of funereal Contemplation
And the Sage returned to Earth
Revived by a measure of surrender
That made her spurn all Earthbound joys.

For the great Joy of ceaseless Contemplation
Took over, adorning her feet with wings that
Carried her back to her true Home at
The Center of the Great whirling Sun,
A Home that transcends all immanence ...
Birth, Death, Rebirth,
Time, Space, and Causality.

Chapter Four

Self ... Imagination, Desires, Thoughts, Body

22

Hymn to Dreamless Sleep

The Sage who longs for Reality
Recognizes Dreamless Sleep as
True rest ... a gift of God and
A presaging mimesis of Nirvana.

Freedom from sense gratification,
Hard earned through moral vigilance,
Expresses itself in the contents and intensity of dreams.
When Reality knocks on the door, vanquishing desires,
Dreams become a ring of whispers
Surrounding the silence of Dreamless Sleep
Until they vanish in the icon of the Divine
Beheld in dreams, when the sleeper dreams of naught else.

But Dreamless Sleep is unearned ...
Inside the rowdy heart of dream infested sleep,
In the mind of each living being,
There hides a God given patch of Dreamless Sleep.
All sentient beings drink the living waters of this Elixir ...
The same unwilled Dreamless Sleep.

Intoxicated by the theater of crowded dreams
In the marketsquare of the thinking mind,
The sleeper sleeps, but does not rest ...
For she straggles far from Reality.
Her dreams are loud ... an admixture of
Internal noise from the dungeon of the subconscious,
External noise from the collective consciousness.

Suddenly, lifted beyond herself ... without effort or merit,
Held aloft by the buoyant Light of Grace ...
Suddenly she is transported ...
Beyond Time, Space and Causality,
Beyond ordinary consciousness
To the Pure Consciousness that hosts Dreamless Sleep.

The Sage who sings this hymn to Dreamless Sleep ...
Draws all who yearn to break free from worldliness
To awaken in Truth ... with body, mind
Nestled in Endless Light ... Reposing in Absolute Being,
Beyond the hymnal silence of Dreamless Sleep.

Like a waterfall, her voice pours forth –
"Oh Holy Sleep! Gift of Grace!
Divine center of noisy slumber,
Supreme harbinger of peace,
Soothing, refreshing sleep!

Who sleeps any more?

Oh Dreamless Sleep! Heart of Slumber,
Where memory halts, imagination stalls,
Light enfolds and silence reigns,
Wrapping the mind in
That shining Constant ... the Ecstatic.

Oh Dreamless Sleep!
You sing a lullaby that lures
The thought infested mind, quivering with multiplicity
Inside the sleeping body, to escape to your Refuge
Beyond the threshold of the Ecstatic ...
For Reality, a glowing Lamp embedded in Dreamless Sleep ...
Emits the aura that is Dreamless Sleep.

Oh holy Sleep!
Enchanter of enchanters,
You are centered by your inmost Shrine –
Where dreams falter, dying their natural death,
Extinguished by their encounter with Reality ...
Exhumed by their double unreality ...
Exhumed because Reality wrings imagination dry,
Cleansing it of desires ... and therefore of dreams.

Oh Holy Sleep!
Manna from heaven ... you are wholly unearned ...
A free gift, you are bestowed equally on all.

Unmerited by meditation, prayer, or virtue
You silence memory, diffuse potential dreams,
And clear away cobwebs of sooty imagination,
For you cradle the mind in true repose.

Oh Dreamless Sleep!
Gentle guardian, tender Light,
You enter the clamor of dream-infested sleep,
To empty the mind of desire,
To bequeath your Light of Auspiciousness,
And put to flight the thinking mind ...
As the power of fancy recoils, dreams fade ...

Like terrified ghosts
Dreams fade as imagination stalls ...
Body and mind repose
In the boundless lap of the Holy Spirit,
Dipping into this solitary common pool of Light
To find relief from frenetic desires.
Partaking of this holy communion, alongside all sentient beings,
Each with equal access to this shared pool of Light,
The thinking mind, exhausted by desire-laden thought, is
Cradled by God, without supplication,
In the same holy state of Dreamless Sleep.

Oh bewitching Mimesis of Death!
Oh Celestial Moment,
When Time dies and Breath deepens,
Touch us! Heal us!"

To the sleeper, Dreamless Sleep answers –
"May every pore in you radiate a healing Light.
In the ambiance of this pure luminosity,
May you realize who you are –
Ultimate Reality, ensconced in five sheaths of the unreal.
And as you vibrate with the Divine Name ...
May your corporeal garment fade.
May the subtle body ensconcing the Real you ...
May this thought infested mind, incapable of silence, fade as well."

But Dreamless Sleep does not possess
The power to confer Self-knowledge ...
No more than a portent of the morally pure
State of *Nirvanic* enlightenment,
Earned by the moral vigilance that overcomes the ego,
Dreamless Sleep, can, at best, give the sleeper
A foretaste of the empathetic body,
Experienced by one who transcends the body
Through strenuous moral purification.
To the ordinary mind, Dreamless Sleep confers repose ...
But to the Seeker, it confers purification.

As Dreamless Sleep deepens in the sleeping Seeker,
Melding body and mind to a sublime melody,
Transporting this Song from the visible to the Invisible,
Sublimating it to a Shining Silhouette ...
As all this happens,
This musical fusion of body and mind grows
Light ... Lissome ... Luminous!

Experienced in the heart, the eyes, the temple,
Beyond male and female, beyond multiplicity,
This shimmering union of body and mind
Is neither body, nor spirit, but a rhapsody of both –
For under the power of Dreamless Sleep,
Body melts in the living shrine of Spirit.

The magnetic Light of Dreamless Sleep
Pushes the Seeker to awaken out of "wakeful" worldliness ...
Refreshes her, by chasing away noisy extraneous sleep –
The chatter of imagination, memory, desires, thoughts.
Not as powerful as the earned *Nirvanic* state of desirelessness, yet
This magnetic Light is potent enough ... to flush out imagination,
Dissolving debris of dreams and nightmares ...
As thought subsides and the last dream fades,
Amidst this subtle Silence, sleep grows illumined –
Vacant, glowing, thought-free ... at long last, a true Refuge!

Now the hermitage of the sleeping body, is
An echo of Pure Felicity ...
A poem rhyming with the rhythm of the universe!

A Light enters each pore of the slumbering body,
Pouring its molten rays, as Spirit seizes, binds, contains,
Purging the body of materiality, multiplicity, visibility.
Light binds each particle in its own fragrant secrecy.

Now integral, chaste, a seat gathered unto itself,
Spilling forth Love, Grace, and Strength,
The sleeping body becomes a Moral Being –
Overflowing with empathy,
It feels the pain of every living being ...
The hunger of the hungry, the sickness of the sick ...
Bathed and refreshed in the deep peace of Divine Love
The heart is hushed ... all desires have thawed into
Resplendent, magnificent Devotion!

And as Grace descends, the Seeker's sleeping body
Sheds tears of awakening, tears of Devotion.
Baptismal tears spill forth as her body rejoices,
Luminous amidst Pure Luminosity.
In this living chorus of body and mind,
The inner eye sees with tenderness ... it sees Beauty.
The inner ear listens with tenderness ... it hears Beauty.
The inner tongue speaks with tenderness ... it utters Beauty.
Magnified by devotion, the seeker's mind overflows with
Rightness and righteousness ... it grows desireless ...
And as the body partakes of this ceaseless feast, it fades ...

Now liberating doubt unleashes Faith,
And the Seeker's fearless mind befriends Death,
For ... to this shining melody of body and mind
Refreshed by Dreamless Sleep,
Death is Awakening!

But the ordinary sleeper awakens to
Mundane consciousness ... a kind of sleep,
Frayed and burdened with the noise of iniquities,
For the magic of Dreamless Sleep has passed away ...
It was unearned ... but will return
Whenever the sleeper sleeps.

23

When Imagination Dies

Like a sinking ship, it heaves ...
A colossal, corroded imagination.

Like a serpent, it writhes ...
A bloated imagination assailed by
Inauspicious thought-vipers that appear as unholy images ...
Spreading their dark aura ... obscuring Pure Consciousness,
Threatening to eclipse empirical reality in a vortex of delusion ...

But as the splendor of Divine Light pierces imagination
Diffusing each grotesque image with the power of Reality,
Infusing healing tinctures of empirical objectivity
Into each specious image in the canvas of imagination,
Shaking the fetid soil of blinding desires off its roots –
As this Light continues to pound,
Imagination grows beautiful, bright, panoramic ...

Now beatified and beautified, yet ...
The power of desire-driven fancy has not vanished ...
Straggling far from Reality, imagination, still too vivid,
Threatens to drown the mind in a miasma of desires.
For this power of fancy, still too flaccid ... needs Light.
The last lingering striae of fancy indicate
An ailing imagination still mired in the unreal ...
Only purified imagination, shorn clean of fancy, is
Worthy of hosting images of the Real ...
Perfected imagination is an empty, unreal canvas,
Replete with unreal forms that receive the Real.

But as the Light ... relentless and forceful,
Pounds the edifice of imagination, it diffuses fancy ...
Like slumbering bats beneath cottage eaves
Desires begin stirring in the mind's dungeons ...
Blinded by the Light of Reality, they fade ...

As Light explodes inside imagination,
Flocks of desires flee the meditating mind ...
From its luminous throne, the divine Spectator
Witnesses these hordes of desires ...
Stumbling ... sprouting wings that force them
To their death in the Light of Reality.
Like moths drawn to their funeral pyre
Desires die by the thousands.

As this blinding Light of Reality eclipses its offspring –
The borrowed light of empirical reality –
Imagination collapses like a pricked balloon ...
And as this higher Light devours its derived mirage,
Revealing empirical reality for what it is –
A Cosmic Illusion conjured by the playful Spectator –
Imagination empties itself of the power of fancy.
Now bereft of desires and shorn of the unreal,
Imagination shrinks to a nugget of derived Light.

At long last redeemed of the fire of fancy,
Sublimated imagination ... an obedient altar of meditation,
Is finally worthy of hosting sensory icons of the Real.
Purified imagination, still an unreal vessel,
Trembles with its limitless contents ...
The endless, incorporeal Light of the Real.

Now probing each chamber of consciousness,
This holiest Light cleans all cobwebs,
Washing all sores ... in dreams, ego, memory,
Bathing these in the Light of Pure Consciousness,
Chasing the subconscious unto oblivion by
Polishing this dungeon until it becomes
Revealed, redeemed, redundant.

And as this living Flame dances in the mind,
Washing every crevice, emptying imagination and memory –
It rejoices, integrating all chambers of consciousness into a whole ...
Vanquishing sooty thought-atoms inherited from past lives
And stored in the subconscious dungeon of the mind ...

Cleansed of the soot of sin,
The mind becomes visible ...
Suddenly the mind is *mindful* ...
The inner Spectator can now see
The objectified mind ... radiant with joy!

And as devotion spreads its fragrance
The ego shrinks to a humble mist-like vessel ...
No longer an identity ... but a fleeting instrument.
And as the Light erupts into molten radiance,
Exulting in the desireless, deathless state,
The mind becomes a near silent hymn of Joy.

24

Imagination Transfigured

Like a damp cloth
Imagination, a noetic fool, hung heavy,
Bloated with desires that beguiled it
Into the ensnaring thralldom of the unreal,
The relative world of *Maya*,
Making it lose its foothold in the Real.

When suddenly, like a flaming Sun
The Divine Name rose on the horizon of the mind.
Ferociously It seized imagination,
Wringing it dry of desire ... of
Its power of fancy that conjured
A sphere of the unreal within the unreal ...

The Divine Name seized imagination
Wringing it dry of its departure and distance
From the Truth that is Reality ...
Turning its direction away from the world of fancy
And the desires that create the contents of fancy ...

The Divine Name seized imagination,
Emptying it of the power to conjure images –
Icons twice removed from Reality –
Converting imagination to a heady
Instrument of meditation ... succinct, still, empty.

Like bats disturbed from their slumber of delusion,
Desires flew out of imagination –
And in this flight each desire carried,
On its one-way journey
A knapsack filled with the power of fancy
Rooted in desire, leaving behind
An empty imagination, refreshed by
The power of true creativity that blossoms
In the endlessness of divine Light.

Imagination now stands still –
An empty, desireless temple,
A fresh cloth dried in the
Sunlight of the Divine Name.

A disciplined imagination
Now shorn of desire and sin,
Is powerful enough to erase
Deluding mists of the unreal
That hang like lingering cobwebs
In nooks and crannies of the deluded mind.

A disciplined imagination
Now shorn of desire and sin,
Ceases to conjure images ...
Free of fancy, free of *Maya*, meditative,
Imagination is now quiet enough
To draw raw materials
From the miasma of the unreal ...
And fashion mist-like vessels of names and forms
Then *receive* (not conjure) images ...
Sublime Forms of the Divine,
First rays of Light beheld in these unreal vessels.

A disciplined imagination
Now shorn of desire and sin,
And shining with glory, possesses in its fold
The power to slice through swirling mists of the unreal,
To reveal the Real in the medium of the unreal
Through myriad divine icons
Received in the shining temple of imagination.

Transfigured ... from noetic fool and tool of desire
To an instrument of desirelessness and self-surrender,
Imagination, first emptied, now replenished
By the Royal Truth on the throne at its center,
This shining imagination becomes the
Gateway to desirelessness.

25

Not Tomb but Tabernacle

The cosmos itself is a body ...
A blessed womb that enfolds
Teeming forms of relative being,
Each rendered visible by its name and form ...
Unreal signatures that shine with
The borrowed Light of Ineffable Reality...

This adorned universe is a temple
Teeming with ornamental smaller bodies ...
It is a tabernacle hosting bodies within bodies
Some spherical, others not, some living, others not,
Some shining, others dark ...

But if there is one common aspect to all bodies ...
To every star, all orbiting orbs ... it is surely this –
No corpus is more than an outer sheath, an echo,
A sedimentation and reification of its subjective spirit ...
And sitting enthroned within the central shrine of each spirit, is
The Royal Spectator, the objective Indwelling Spirit ...

Two spirits dwell in each corpus ...
The faint individual spirit and its glowing archetype ...
The Great Spirit, of which the smaller is a distorted reflection.
For every corpus in the divine cosmos is ensouled
By the all knowing, ubiquitous Great Spirit.

Like a flame flickering in an opaque lamp,
Spirit sparkles inside each body,
Enabling each to blossom to its
Highest teleological potential ... as a Somatic Tabernacle.

Each thought that arrives in the cavern of the mind,
Leaves its signature upon the human body.
A frenzy of appetites churn the living body, at its lowest
Turning it into a catacomb that entombs the Living Spirit,
Obfuscating Spirit in the tentacles of matter.

But at its highest ...
When the smaller human spirit immolates itself
In the living fire of the Great Spirit within,
And this inner Light illumines all the senses,
Snaring the appetites, sublimating each unto oblivion,
Then the same human body actualizes its potential,
Becoming the supreme Tabernacle of Spirit,
By surrendering the obstructing opacity of matter
At the altar of Spirit ...

As the smaller individual spirit journeys towards
Its noble Archetype, the Great Spirit, by –
Harnessing the appetites, disciplining the senses,
Sublimating the raw passions, diffusing the raging desires,
Elevating these to the better desires –
It reaches a peak where it offers its last desire and sin
Upon its own funeral pyre, immolating itself
By leaping into the final Flame of the Great Spirit ...

Bereft of somatic awareness,
No longer entombed by the body,
The individual spirit transcends its breathing body,
Immolating itself in the Living Fire of the Great Spirit.

Like a common Flame shining in assorted lamp wicks,
This Great Spirit dwells in assorted bodily tabernacles,
Illumining each eternally,
By redeeming its mayhem of the temporal
With Its own touch of the Eternal.

But it is only when the smaller human spirit
Consciously imbibes the Great Spirit,
Extinguishing itself in this divine Origin,
That the lamp loses its outer contours
In the uncontainable living Light it seeks to contain ...
The purified Love Body, a throbbing temple,
Now emerges, glowing with inner Light ...
A Light that transcends its body, animating it,
Transforming this tomb to a Tabernacle ...

This shining Great Spirit that devoured
The little individual spirit
Now enjoys the somatic felicity of
A disciplined body, shorn of lust ...
An empathetic Love Body ...
An unobtrusive Tabernacle that does not
Trouble Spirit with its material presence.

For the body has now reached its
Original purpose, actualizing the *telos*
Archived in its very make-up ...

For the somatic self is constructed in its minutiae –
As a vehicle of Enlightenment, a Song of Meditation
As a benediction of the Great Spirit,
Which sports alone, rejoicing in Itself
Through Its numberless glowing somatic altars.

For the somatic self is constructed in its minutiae –
To be a Love Body ... a seat of Empathy,
A noble temple, a Tabernacle that echoes
Each seismic tremor of the ascending spirit ...

For the somatic self is constructed in its minutiae –
To reach its full potential as the glorious Love Body,
Cleansed of appetites, a living lyre, whereupon
The Great Spirit plays Its song celestial.

For the somatic self is constructed in its minutiae –
To weep with the sorrowful, rejoice with the joyful ...
For it is a tangible halo of the meditating spirit,
For it is a tablet that receives signatures of the ascending spirit
In its spinal activity, and tingling brain.

For the somatic self is constructed in its minutiae –
To be an intricate mapping, built and constructed
Not for appeasing inordinate appetites,
But for the meditative ascent from
Reflected spirit to archetypal Great Spirit ...

For the somatic self is constructed in its minutiae –
To be living, breathing, empathetic, loving ...
An adorned Tabernacle of the Great Spirit,
That dips ceaselessly into its Source,
Drawing life rhythmically by breathing ...
Inhaling this Supreme Elixir, exhaling the same Elixir.

The inhalation, betrothed to the exhalation,
Together, they anchor this glowing Tabernacle
To its origin and parent ... the Great Spirit,
For each salubrious breath is
The umbilical cord that anchors
The Love Body to the Great Spirit ...

For the body was built, not to entomb spirit,
And matter was never meant to rule Spirit ...
Nor Spirit matter ...
Rather, matter is a halo of Spirit ...
Tangible matter expresses Spirit ...

Spirit uses this Love Body – a powerhouse,
And the holiest of all tabernacles ...
To recreate Creation.
Spirit uses this living Temple to
Heal with a touch, redeem with a look,
Supplant sin with virtue ...
And with its listening
And its profound power of understanding,
Spirit uses this living Temple to
Supplant sorrow with Joy.

26

Bridge of Desires

As the Sage stood on the green bow-shaped Bridge,
With latticed rails, she looked into the
Dark, swirling, baptismal waters of Renunciation,
Flanked by graceful foliage.
Tall thickets of stately trees garlanded the lake.
Marring this serene scene was the parched pile of refuse,
At the foot of the Bridge.
But redeeming this mountain of litter
Was a luminous ladder installed at the upper end of the Bridge,
A ladder that disappeared in the cottonwool clouds above,
Leading to a shining thralldom of graded heavens,
Well beyond the visible material cosmos.

Far above the heavens,
There ruled a giant Sun of Truth,
Illumining all that becomes
In the silent procession of Becoming.
And as the Sage looked hither, thither ...
Wondering why she was there,
The Bridge spoke to her –
"I am," it said in a sotto voice, "the Bridge of Desires."

How strange ... that while each desire is itself
A bridge between the inner and the outer,
The collective hive of desires, parading in a procession,
Dwells upon yet another Bridge ...
The alluring Bridge of Desires, a continuum
That leads from the ominous to the auspicious.

And as her eyes looked at the sweeping curve of the Bridge
She saw that it was, in truth, a fossil of
The searing procession of desires, with every two desires
Punctuated by an interval of earthly happiness
When the mind reposes in the peace of
An unearned, momentary desirelessness.

But how different from this undeserved, temporary desirelessness
Were the two contrary, clashing forms of desirelessness,
That flanked the procession of desires,
One at each end of this Bridge –
The ominous, temporal incapacity for desire,
A dark desirelessness caused by violence ...
Located at the sobering foot of the Bridge –
And opposing this ... the auspicious unselfish, eternal
Transcendence of ego-laden desire
Located beyond the upper end of the Bridge.

For leading up the ladder, and
Exceeding the shining heavens above,
There glowed an ethereal desirelessness
At the epicenter of the regal Sun of Truth.
This eternal, *earned* transcendence of desire was
The noble essence of the Sun of Truth.
The Bridge of Desires therefore links
An eerie, desolate desirelessness, choking with hidden desires
To the shining, joyful desirelessness that
Rises like a phoenix, from the ashes of desire.
It connects the two unmatching bookends of desirelessness
Through the ever moving convoy of desires, in between ...
A convoy punctuated by flashing moments of unearned desirelessness ...
Restful moments that interrupt each discursive pair of desires.

This Bridge is therefore a transmutation of
The love for power to the Power of Love –
It is a metamorphosis of the aching desire to be loved
To the aching desire to give Love –
It is a transition from anger to Joy,
From hatred to Love, from the ominous to the auspicious.

The Bridge of Desires spans two opposite moral states,
The first, a desireless recoiling from worldliness, and
A drowning in the bottomless angry pit of the ego ...
And the second, a desireless transcendence of worldliness
Unto an expunging of the ego.

At one end, arising from the parched pile of refuse
At the foot of the Bridge, there is a selfish desirelessness.
But once this refuse is overcome, the convoy of desires emerges
From its dark burrows to the spotlight of awareness in the healing mind.
The Bridge begins with selfish desires, that blend into moderate desires,
Tapering off with muted, but vivid unselfish desires
At the upper end of the Bridge, at the foot of the ladder leading to the heavens.

Each desire gave the mind a false meaning and value ...
Both the moral march of desires and the better desires were
Golden petals so vital to earthly happiness ...
Yet each was also chimerical, adding to the miasma of earthly life ...
For when the Sage looked upwards, beyond the ladder to the shining heavens,
She saw the trailing smoke of scintillating desires, grow refined and refreshed
As it entered the imposing gates of the shining constellation of heavens.
But far above this noble assemblage of heavens, at the gates of Truth,
This smoke of desires vanished into a blazing halo of Desirelessness.

Desires are like fireflies
So alluring, so beguiling,
They rise in sparkling swarms.
They fade in sparkling swarms.

At the foot of the Bridge,
The spirit withdraws from the empirical world,
Drowning in the whirlpool of its native wrath,
Sinking into despondency, for it has departed from Truth.
This forlorn, rootless state of mind
Makes the spirit rupture with
An unexpected gush of alluring desires,
Like the parched desert gushes with
The mirage of false crystalline water.

Still drowning in wrath, by the parched pile of refuse
The anchorless soul experiences a
"Desireless" mind, choking with concealed desires,
As it withdraws from the world
Moving first inward, then downward.
Drowning in its own torpid ego-swamp,
The spirit so starved loses the ability to desire.

It becomes unaware that it possesses desires ...
No desires are visible at the foot of this Bridge.

But once Divine Light pours into the mind
In the excess of Grace, It illumines
Every thought tendril, eliciting hidden desires,
Banishing despondency, orienting this dreary mind
Away from its ego ... turning it in the opposite direction
Towards its native inner Light.

Divine Light thus *educates* the dreary mind
By orienting it away from the darkness of desire
Towards the great surrender of desirelessness
Before the great Sun of Truth,
Shining above the heavens ... but also within each mind.

But this does not happen directly ...

For first, healed somewhat from its inner wrath,
This mind can afford a dose of worldliness,
Now gaining the power to spill outwards
Through a desire-laden, passion-stricken grasp of the
Empirical world ... snatching and clutching,
Grabbing and seizing ... ambitious, curious
Ego driven, externalized, bereft of Self-knowledge ...
Yet subjecting the searing world of multiplicity
To avid scrutiny through science and technology.
For the outward eye ... bemused, deluded,
Longs to be trapped in the ensnaring
Worldliness of the world, so it can escape
The raw boiling cauldron that is its native "I."

The raging libido spills out of the ego
Into the empirical world ...
Like forceful flood waters that refashion the land ...
Each libidinal outpouring is driven by a
Life-saving desire that prevents the libido from withdrawing
From the empirical world and drowning in inner wrath.

But after its desire-driven outpouring of libido
Into the world of nature and civilization

Is honed by ethics ... which mitigates desire ...
And after it has lost itself in a flurry of activity
In this enticing empirical world, drowning in *Maya*,
Like moths enthralled by leaping flames ...
And after it has been sizzled by
The searing flames of worldliness and cynicism ...
Only then does the chastened mind return home,
Its desires bettered ethically ...
For it has now traversed the Bridge of Desires
That spills outwards, then inward,
Then, trembling with devotion to Truth
The mind, now ennobled, prepares to ascend upwards ...

But first, it stumbles upon the last lingering desire
At the upper end of the Bridge of Desires –
This is the flaming desire for
Recognition, renown, name and fame.

Yet ruling from beyond the constellation of heavens,
And also from deep inside the human heart,
Shining Truth has not ceased its enchanting call ...
Entreating all who have wandered away
To return to their natural home in Truth.
Like the ocean that recalls its waves at ebb tide
Truth recalls its offspring at the ebb tide of desires.

Standing still at the upper end of the Bridge of Desires,
Clutching at its rugged rails, as her mind muses ...
Struggling between worldly renown and heavenly repose ...
The Sage searches her pocket to find this last lingering
Self-directed desire ... the hunger for name and fame,
Fluttering among unselfish desires, which, nevertheless
Tug at the opaque ego-screen that blinds her mind.

And as her supremely serene mind looks upwards
At the heavenly Star of Truth ...
And as the Sage prepares to ascend the ladder
Leaving forever the alluring Bridge of Desires ...
She empties her pockets and flings into the
Shining waters of Renunciation
All lingering cravings ... even ethical desires ...
Especially the desire for name and fame.

Now, in one leap, her mind escapes the
Enchaining Bridge of Desires,
Flying into the limpid night sky,
Free as air, having shed its
Twin weights of desire and sin.
Flying high upon its luminous wings of
Dispassion and Discrimination,
This desireless spirit returns home to
The Truth Supreme ruling above the
Shining constellation of graded heavens.

Desireless, free from sin, released from
The asphyxiating cage of the ego
This pilgrim-mind rejoices in itself,
Having shed all appearance,
Having blossomed into its
Innate, eternal shared Essence,
Reposing as the whirling Sun of Truth
Shining ferociously, illumining everything
Both within and without each being.

Having escaped the death caused by
Desire, sin, and a smothering ego,
The Sage is alive at last,
Rejoicing in her flight from
The relative to Absolute Being –
The fountainhead of True Love.

Discrimination with Dispassion

Like a floating candle, the ripened soul
Rises in the dark night of the world,
Illumined by the might of her virtues,
Borne by ethereal wings –
The twin virtues of discrimination and dispassion.

More than a mere wing, discrimination bequeaths gifts –
It kindles the eye of the mind, enabling it to discern
Between good and evil ... between the Real and the unreal.
Discrimination, an echo of Conscience,
Reveals to the soul, its God given free will,
Guided and circumscribed by a vigilant Divine Will.

But no soul can fly on one ... or even two wings
Unless the two cooperate ...

In the end, no soul is wingless, no soul has isolated wings ...
Every soul has the hidden potential to soar with strength,
For its two wings are sympathetic and symbiotic ...
Dispassion enhances discrimination,
Discrimination sublimates the passions.
Discrimination without dispassion degenerates to judgmentalism,
Dispassion without discrimination degenerates to apathy, insensibility.

Bolstered by dispassion, discrimination begins to shine
Like a lighthouse in shark infested waters.
Discrimination becomes a beacon of hope ...
The soul can now discern and adjudicate
Without hating that which is evil and unreal.

With discrimination bolstering it,
Dispassion becomes tranquility,
The supreme state of Equipoise between –
Extremes fueled by the stormy passions,
Extremes that tempt us,
Drowning us in the pairs of opposites,
Making us falter far from Equilibrium.

Who am I?

The Sage looks into
The Great Mirror of Life
To search for herself ...
What does she see,
But a blank silhouette,
Invisible to the bare eye.

The Mirror does not lie ...

For, the Sage is ...
Neither body, nor mind,
Neither ego, nor perception,
Neither memory, nor imagination,
Neither opinion, nor knowledge,
Neither desire, nor dream ...
Certainly, she is not thought.

And as she peers closer
Her eyes singed with thirst for Self-knowledge,
She reaches beyond body and mind
To find herself one with the Mirror of Life,
Now emptied of all reflections ...

For ...
She is the common Flame that
Binds all beings in the ringing
Melody of the One.

Chapter Five

Love

29

Not love but Love

A thousand skeletons spill forth,
Breaking the embankment.

They thirst ... they take ... they hoard ...
They have nothing to give.
Deluded by the mirage of bounty
In the shadow worlds,
They crave forever ... like hungry ghosts.

In the horizon rises
The glittering sun of desire –
A phantom sun that gives nothing ...
Only beckons ... with a cruel bait ...
It entices with the promise of love ...

What love is this?
Is it that unselfish communion,
Where the self and the other
Bridge the gulf by
Knowing each other with friendship ...
Or is it a carnal intrusion,
A cruel caricature of Gentle Love?

Distending the universal mirage of *Maya*,
The sun of desire beckons through
Bodies, bodies ... still more bodies –
Bodies of clothes, cars, products,
Bodies blatant, bodies intruding,
Possessions that can be bartered, sold, exchanged ...
Then suddenly discarded, with the fury of boredom.

Beneath the blazing sun of desire
That darkens the worlds with its tinsel light,
A pile of litter rises to the sky –
Possessions tossed away with the disdain of abundance ...
Cars, clothes, toys, furniture ... an electronic jungle.

Anything with form can allure ... and be craved –
But also discarded ... with disdain.

Beneath this roaring junk,
Beneath this mountain of litter,
Beneath this ossifying object consciousness,
There is a bedrock of broken bodies
Famished for love –
Animated bodies that no longer
Discern between sentience and insentience.

Suddenly they creep out –
The once broken bodies
Gaze intently at the tinsel sun of desire ...
Their eyes streaming strength,
They laugh aloud
For they have detected the truth ...
This glittering orb is a mirage!

Ignited by the Light within,
They stand unyielding
Before the relentless call of desire.
Turning their backs to shadows forever,
They renounce the unreal ...
For they thirst for the Real –
Not craving, not tossing and turning,
No longer restless and tempestuous,
Not caught in the fury of boredom.
No longer expanding the inner void,
They stand tall ...
Ignited by the Light within.

No longer hiding loneliness
By cramming the yawning inner chasm,
With bodies and yet more bodies –
For now there is no obsolescence –
They stand proud ...
Ignited by the Light within.

Overflowing with Self-respect,
Discarding all finite husks of infinite Love,

Discovering the futility of this lower love,
They discern between Love and love ...

For they have plunged into
The all shining Infinite Ocean of the Real ...
That limitless, eternal Essence, buried deep within –
Its resplendence shining forth like a thousand suns.
It pours forth Its munificent Love,
Illumining all worlds, devouring the sun of desire
Cleansing all desire to cleave,
Fusing all into a silent mass of Radiance.

Total Light, Halo of Love,
The Real cleans and heals ...
The Real floods the heart with
Abiding Joy.

30

What is Love?

What is love but a throbbing pain,
A hole in the heart, a loss of self,
An arrival into
The thorn and thistle of the untamed wild ...

What is love but blind intoxication,
A flight into delusion,
A tumble into the mirage of the unreal ...

The cesspool of ego enshrouds ...
Eclipsing the living Flame
Enshrined in the altar of the heart.

What is love but an illusory escape from
The catchments of hatred
Encrusting this Flame.
What indeed is lower love but a lower death ...

We are compelled to spill forth and
Engage in love,
For if we recoil from the mirage of
The empirical world,
We sink in languor, drowning in ego,
Sucked by the whirlpool of narcissism.

What therefore is love
But a flight from the cage of your ego,
To the encaging ego of the beloved.
What indeed is love but
A suicide in the torpid
Ego-swamp of the beloved ...

What is finite love, but
A search for a mirror ...
A search for the self that belies

The search for true Self-knowledge
For it appears to unlock the cage of your ego
Only to lock you in the cage of the beloved's ego ...
What indeed is love but the act of dying
By leaping into the mirror that *is* the beloved ...
And drowning in the mirage of your
Own haunting reflection.
What is this lower love
But a deformed refraction of
The very Heart of Truth –
The highest Love that shines at the pinnacle ...
Like a distant star we long to reach ...

Every lower love is
A vicarious search for the Divine.
Every finite love is
A vicarious search for the Infinite ...
A roundabout search for the highest Self,
An indirect bridge to the
Shining Center of the layered,
Centripetal immanent lower self ...

Once you ascend the sacred mountain of Love
Relinquishing every lower love,
The distortion vanishes when,
Like a touchstone, this highest teleological Love
Becomes transforming ... as you die to the world ...
And awaken to the Light within ...

31

Trembling Love

A balm of Altruism rules
The glowing peak of the mountain of Love
Shining forth ... as its radiant halo ...
But whirling at the base of this Holy Hill
In breathless despair, are the numberless acts of
Specious, addictive love, bemused and bemusing,
Teeming with the dust and din of selfishness.

Ruling this sacred mountain
Is a trembling Love – the first song of Piety ...
An unselfish, incorporeal Love that transcends the particular ...
An abstract detached Love, to be gifted without bias,
With nobody favored, nobody disfavored ...
A Love that attracts a multitude of beloveds
Without the sclerotic pall of raw concupiscence ...
A cornucopia of Love that finds the Divine in every beloved,
Like the bee, maddened with longing, finds nectar in every flower.

Ruling this sacred mountain
Is a trembling Love – the first song of Piety ...
A Love that hones the eye, until, like an arrow,
The eye pierces each mask (without intruding)
To reveal the radiant Divinity throbbing in each heart
In the multitude of beloveds ...
Each beloved is a mask worn by the Compassionate One,
And the multitude of beloveds is a bouquet of radiant flowers.

Ruling this sacred mountain
Is a trembling Love – the first song of Piety ...
A song that extinguishes consciousness of the body,
Rousing the self from its temporal slumber
In the inchoate, entombing state of embodiment ...
A song that purifies the senses until they touch
Every wave of living Light encrusted by opacity ...

Ruling this sacred mountain
Is a trembling Love – the first song of Piety ...
A song that attracts like a magnet
The centripetal dance of the self, athirst for Self-knowledge.
Love leads the pilgrim, through layers of opaque identities,
To the concealed shrine of the luminous true Self.

Ruling this sacred mountain
Is a trembling Love – the first song of Piety ...
A song that collects
The flying debris of relative being.

Ensconced in the cavern of a "now,"
Like a pearl embedded in an oyster,
Each relative being rides the crest of the
Twin waves of Time and Becoming.
Like the wind gathering flying leaves,
Like the shepherd gathering his sheep,
Love gathers in its embrace
Every being, every "now,"
Turning all into a silent shining One!

For Love is the
Throbbing awareness that
You and I are one – not by fusing us together,
For Love does not convert one to the other.
Love unites us at the level of
A superseding, harmonizing One, or
The universal Self revealed by
Dissolving the blinding hill of ego!

32

Glad Stranger

As she sits in the sun drenched alcove
Beneath the canopy of
The gentle Jacaranda, a Purple Flame,
The caressing wind arrives –
Gentle zephyr, messenger of the gods –
And as the grass trembles with unspeakable joy,
She sees before her mind's eye, visual echoes of many loves ...

Faint faces appear from the distant past,
Nameless adults who cradled her in her infancy,
Faces that enkindle memory-flames of
The sweet grace of love, each love, a pure gift,
A candle with a living flame,
Unique, invaluable, incomparable, immeasurable.

And as these perishable memories of perishable love
Emerge from alcoves in the far flung corners of
Her amphibious consciousness ...
As these memories of love arrive, imbuing her mind with
Their false strength of tenacious attachment,
Mimicking in vain the robust morning sun, which
Strengthens the horizon it rises upon ...
As these memories arrive as a grandiloquent
Annunciation of attachment that surprises her unprepared mind,
Like the first crocuses surprise the spring they announce ...
As these past loves arrive, betrothed to one another
In their baptismal procession, flooding her mind
With their sweet fragrance, numbing loneliness,
Connecting her to all that exists by
Imperceptible golden threads that imprison –
Enriching her, imbuing with meaning
The raw existential forlornness of her life ... yet incarcerating her ...

Amidst all this *seeming* joy
Suddenly she is jolted ...

For ... in the chamber of her consciousness
Each golden love has left
A sooty footprint of pain, a needling sadness,
A patch of emptiness, a touch of delusion
That hides the silent passage of Time
And the blunt blatant fact of Death.
Each love now appears in a new light –
Despairing, stooping low, weighed down
By the enormous burden of its forlorn shadow.
For tied to each love is the grim hatred
That follows as its unfailing shadow.
Ordinary love obeys these laws ...
To love something, is to hate its opposite.
To love fanatically is to hate the same object.

Each golden love lassos the beloved in its
Glittering noose of attachment that ties us to Earth,
Deluding us into thinking we possess the power to
Stall the treadmill of nomadic Time –
To strike roots upon ever changing Earth ...
Like two executioners, Death and Time
Link hands in a grim camaraderie,
To make of us, perpetual wanderers,
With no power to pause enough
To strike roots upon this transient Earth.

Every love distracts from our raw aloneness –
For we are born alone, we shall die alone,
And in the interregnum between birth and death,
Betrothed as we are to a myriad feverish loves –
We succumb to the delusion that we are not alone.

And as the Sage stands firm and strong
Beneath that swirl of purple, the gentle Jacaranda,
She shakes off every love ... past, present and future.
She pays heed to the inexorable ticking moments of
The life span bestowed upon her and
She listens for the adumbrating
Call of her unique, unshared Death.

And from this long rumination,
The Sage emerges a Glad Stranger,

Prepared to journey alone ... yet never alone,
For she ascends alone to that great Alone.

Unlike the huddled masses, who cleave together,
Enjoying the delusion of their shared togetherness
Like addicts share addictions, reveling in the particular,
Oblivious of the universal, drowning themselves in
Alluring spotlights of perishable, particular loves,
The Glad Stranger is a harbinger of true Love,
For she has died to the world only to be reborn
In a state of true empathy and detachment.

Now dead to all earthly ties –
A loving Spectator, she has, at long last
The Power to enter the world, with
Infusing intimacy that does not intrude.
Now never alone, even when solitary,
She is in spirit always one with all.

Her solitude is crowded.
Her solitude is loving.
For to the Glad Stranger
Nobody is a stranger.

Having died to the world and transcended the body,
The Glad Stranger loves with unselfish detachment ...
Far away from the multiplicity of beloveds,
She is therefore close enough to touch each
With the Life giving caress of detachment.
She loves with truth ... with wide eyed objectivity,
She loves with distance ... with impartiality.
Her spotlight of imperishable universal Love
Encompasses every being,
For now no love is a particular alluring spotlight
With the power to entrap ...
No love has the power to delude her into forgetting
The stark solitude of her life ... or the stark truth
That the march of her life to the Door of Death ... is
As existentially solitary as is her Death.

Cured forever of the aching need to be loved,
The Glad Stranger recognizes the One in

Each earthly love, and when this
Perishable love vanishes, she is not dismayed,
For she knows that she is betrothed forever
To the One who loves her forever
Through myriad finite instruments, each
Blessed enough to be, for the moment,
The hallowed conduit of this
Imperishable Love from the One.

With her horizontal Love
Now a consecrated residue of
Her vertical Love for the One,
The Glad Stranger is a harbinger of
True Love ... a lionized Love
With the power to vanquish
Every sharp stalactite of anger,
Formed from deposits of desire,
Accrued over many lives, in the long
Meandering March of Transmigration.

As the Glad Stranger sits in that lovely alcove,
Beneath the purple Jacaranda ...
She is radiantly free in the enticing world of multiplicity,
For her many perishable loves have become
The imperishable One, shining with omnipresence,
To be loved in its myriad forms ... human or otherwise.

Now, as she looks at the gentle Jacaranda, at
The willowy grass beneath her feet, at
The bumble bee visiting his flowers,
The sloping meadow of shimmering green,
The hillside so tranquil,
The goatherd and his meandering goats ...
As she looks at all these beings –
Some lamenting, others rejoicing
Some friends, others enemies –
She recognizes the same shining One
In this heaving mass of name and form.

Freed by the magic of Renunciation,
The Glad Stranger is not *of* this world,
Because she dwells deep *within* this world.

33

Anger quenched by Love

Billows of anger rise like dark mushroom clouds
From sharp torrents of desire-arrows,
Each a bubble of delusion that coalesces with others
To burst forth in a thunderous flare of anger comprising –
Dense, concentrated desire and departure from Truth.

When the soul loses its eternal anchor
In the gentle loving One – or the Truth that rules
From yonder ... beyond good and evil ...
When the soul thus meanders away from Truth,
It unleashes in itself torrents of desire,
Each seduced by the pall of untruth in the
Lost, fading soul.

These torrents of desire then transmute to anger,
Like the rushing rain transmutes to stalactites.

As anger smolders,
Churning the soul with grinding motion,
Robbing it of its share of Divine Intelligence,
It ignites on the soul-floor
Stalagmites of sadness – heavy, dreary, inauspicious.

Starved of Light, the soul grows famished
For it forgets its source of Life –
Eternal Love, a central shrine ever aflame ...
In fact ... a Flame ensconcing Flame –
A Love-chalice already aflame and
Brimming with the living flames of
Forgiveness and penance for the enemy.

The moorless soul forgets
This living Flame of Love
And the Flame within Flame –
The Flame of forgiveness.

But Love does not forget the soul ...
When Redemption begins Its act of Grace
And the soul begins its pilgrimage home ...
It returns to its Anchor, its will no longer free
But enchained in golden chains to the divine will.
For Love takes charge of the soul,
Reminding it of its eternal nature –
That inmost shrine, luminous flame of Divine Love
Standing still amidst the hurry of temporality.

And as Love radiates Its glow,
It melts every stalactite of anger,
Dissolving all scythes of sadness that have
Mushroomed on the bruised soul-floor.

And as Love causes the soul to blossom –
Devouring every desire,
Extinguishing scorching anger
Until there is no temper to lose –
The soul becomes a mass of radiant Love –
Boundless, blissful, silent.

The heedful soul now
Lithe with Light and Love,
Guards its gates – fending off
The twin knaves of anger and sadness.

34

Trinitarian Flame of Love

This world of living multiplicity,
This carnival of living differences,
This moving convoy of beings –
Some sentient, others insentient
Some natural, others synthetic –
This vibrant procession of Becoming,
Immersed in the grand endlessness of Time,
This living arc of the discrete manifold ...
All this, a luminous parade of the
One and same, undivided, eternal Light
Shining ferociously within each being
Yet concealed by the opacity of
Its materiality, body consciousness,
And wakeful slumber.

For no living being, opiated by
The enchanting worldliness of the world
Can be aware of its inner Light.

This common Light, shining ubiquitously in the
Teeming trillion inmost shrines, whether sentient or not –
One installed in each being, like the same eternal flame
In a multitude of temporal lamps – is the Real Absolute Substratum
That sustains upon Its serene, infinite bosom,
The burden of the relative existence of the unreal.

And what is this Light?
What indeed are the trillion steadfast flames
In the trillion restless shrines, each shining like
An eternal candle frozen in the temporal?

What are these flames but
The tri-layered leaping flame of Love,
With compassion, its outermost tangible flame,
Forgiveness, its middle translucent flame,
And as for its inmost transparent flame,

The essence that defines it,
What can this be but God's unending Love,
Shining in the inmost heart of each being,
Enlivening, enthralling every being, but also
Letting Itself be transmuted to the
Living, leaping piety each being exudes
Towards the Divine.

For, the love *from* God is the love *for* God.
The downward flow is the upward flow.
The simplicity of the Divine
Is the simplicity of piety ...

The first two outer layers of compassion and forgiveness
Are the consecrated remains of the third essential Love.
They are the sanctified residues that remain
When the first Love cascading down from the
Fountainhead of the Divine turns upwards, offered as
The living liniment of the creature's
Soulful devotion to the Divine.

This Trinitarian Flame of Love, shining in each being
Mitigates the false glare of the unreal, which
Presumes to compete with the all living Light of Reality.

For, when the awakening being recognizes
This Trinitarian Flame ...
Unaware that it is Flame recognizing Flame ...

When the awakening being awakens *as* this
Trinitarian Flame, erupting with divine Love ...

When the awakening being no longer
Seeks to know its highest Self
For it now *is* this highest Self ...

At this auspicious Moment of God
As it awakens as Supreme Reality,
It recognizes eternally,
The supreme unreality of
The alluring carnival of worldliness.

For deliberate awakening *as* the Trinitarian Flame of Love ...
This conscious act of Self Realization is
The ultimate, fullest entrance into
The whole tapestry of History ... or
The procession of the worldliness of the world,
Distributed ubiquitously across Time and History.

This grand awakening as the Trinitarian Flame of Love
Extinguishes the false glare of worldliness,
Just as the glorious Sun puts to shame
All garish city lights.

When the dream is extinguished, revealing the Real,
All that shines forth as the solitary object-free Subject
Is the infinite, all illumining Trinitarian Flame,
Spilling forth Its Love.

35

Kindred Souls

When Love arrives in the desolate heart –
Like a steadfast flame that snuffs out anger ...
Like the green oasis that refreshes parched sands ...

When Love arrives in the forlorn heart –
Like the morning sun that fulfills the horizon,
Like the lilies that adorn still waters ...

When Love arrives in the anguished heart –
Like the lush spring that fulfills bleak winter,
Like the butterfly that fulfills the caterpillar ...
Its ultimate Other ...

When Love thus arrives ...
Love spills out
Inundating all the worldly worlds.

Like the molten sunlight that slices through frost,
Love, purged of the carnal,
Slices through the ephemeral worldliness of the world.
By the power of Its empathy, Love unlocks each soul ...
Gaining entrance, without carnal intrusion ...
Communing, connecting,
Weaving this forlorn Universe into a web of Empathy,
That turns every being into a Kindred Soul.

Unlike the scientist who casts a web of taxonomy
To "catch" the cosmos in her noetic net,
Giving each heavenly body a utilitarian name
That destroys its inmost music,
Making it shudder in the tentacles of taxonomy ...
Unlike this scientist, Love melds together in waves of charity
The sentient with the insentient, the wild with the tame.
Love turns this forlorn Universe into
An extended "we" that adumbrates the great "I."

Brimming with the universal Love that binds Kindred Souls,
This integrated "we" quells alienation – allowing no strangers ...
For the boundless pale of universal Love permits no pariahs.

Now the stars, the moon, and the distant comets,
Every festive constellation and all living beings
Chorus in their joyful oneness,
This eternal hymn to divine Love.

36

Love was Born

Far away in a little cottage, with its
Red corrugated roof, adobe walls,
Adorned with clambering Wisteria
And quiet smoke curling out of
Its solitary chimney ...

Far away in a little cottage
By the deep dark forest
With the sound of a tinkling waterfall
Floating over the distant hills
Like a song arriving from another life ...

Far away in a little cottage
With its long, sun drenched verandah
Adorned with gay orchids ... emblems of Joy ...
Hanging from the brown wooden beam ...

Far away in a little cottage,
With its verdant garden,
Bobbing dahlias, sweet roses
Clementine, and the gentle jacaranda,
Overflowing with purple flowers ...

One day, far away in this little cottage,
Love was born ...
When the chimerical "beauty" of
Names and forms vanished in shame
Before the resplendent Beauty of the One
Shining forcefully through every name and form
As the grain of Truth concealed in each ...

Far away a little cottage was transfigured
When brilliant rays from the Sun of Love
Entered its bay windows, stopping Time,
Piercing each heart, blurring the distinction
Between Spirit and matter, melding all,

Turning the cottage, its flowers and garden,
Its enchanted residents, into a mass of
Eternal radiance, desireless and throbbing
To the tune of a celestial chime.

Far away in a little cottage
Eternal Love was born, from
The ashes of conquered Time
And with Love ...
Peace arrived, Joy arrived.

Chapter Six

Virtue, Beauty

37

Stairway of Virtues

For lo ...
Amidst the limpid silence of the universe
Where the air is hushed and the heavens stand still
As they snuff out the eerie night of the graded hells,
All gloom vanishes as a song pours down from
The Infinite Light, beyond the created worlds,
Drenching the mind absorbed in its moral vigil,
Nudging it to unbolt its doors to a wondrous sight ...
To the vision of the retinue of shining virtues
Entering the garden of the mind
In a stately procession, upon the onset of this Rhapsody.

Each virtue – a golden nugget of goodness,
Has the power to erase its twin-vice.
For the virtues escort us to *Brahman* –
That shining virginal pasture of Truth,
Ruling from beyond good and evil.

Every virtue is an ornate eye with which
The mind beholds the Divine ...
Yet this same eye is also that with which
The Divine knows the created worlds.

Every virtue is therefore a twofold
Noetic-ocular doorway through which the
Chamber of the Divine and the
Chamber of the mortal
Behold one another in loving embrace.

At first the graceful virtues pirouette to
The rhythm of the divine rhapsody
Cascading from above.
Then they stand, one upon the other
Creating a shining stairway of ascending eyes –
A gleaming noetic-ocular ladder

That leads from the ego to the Universal Self –
The Truth that rules from beyond good and evil.

Shining at the pinnacle of
This radiant stairway,
As its crowning glory ...
Omnipresent ... everywhere and nowhere,
Rules the resplendent Universal Self.

The virtues are separate ... yet related –
For no virtue can substitute for another ...
Yet, the intoxication of divine contagion
Compels a kinship –
The virtues grow kindred ...
Each virtue leads to the other.

But the stairs in this living stairway
Are not petrified into a frozen hierarchy
For the role of the Mother Virtue
Varies by the soul
As does the choice of
Each virtue that forms a stair
In the stairway of the soul.

The moral needs of each soul are unique,
Its coffer of virtues is unique –
For its moral state is unique ...
For a soul's lacunae determine
Which casket of medicinal virtues it needs,
As bestowed by God.

Yet some virtues remain universally
More spiritual than others –
Those with the power to subsume
The dimmer virtues ...
For they have received a greater measure of
The Light of Truth shining yonder ...
Beyond good and evil ...

Overflowing with the Light of Truth
The permanent and universal Mother Virtue is

A divine Love ... universal, just ...
Ruling from afar ... from beyond good and evil –
A tri-colored Love irradiating three shining rays,
Each, a manifestation of Exemplary Love ...
The Light of detached compassion,
The Light of unselfishness,
The Light of forgiveness.

This Living Light of Love ...
A Mother Virtue that gives birth to
Other virtues that follow in its train ...
Is yet also their Daughter ...
For the faintest practice of any virtue
Bequeaths Truth ...
Extinguishes anger, quenches insolence,
Bestows pure inborn Love.

And as the power of Love
Suffuses with Light and Life,
The temporal pastures of the mind,
Spreading its hue of unalloyed Joy,
Thoughts sprint up the Stairway of Virtues ...

Like bees gleaning nectar from brilliant flowers,
Thoughts glean Light from the fragrant virtues ...
Thereupon, sprouting wings at the top of that Stairway –
Soaring high, flying unbound to the
Serene, saffron firmament of the
Infinite incandescent mind, where they shine –
Hosts of radiant thought stars, bathing the mind
In the tranquil Light of the God given luminous virtues.

38

Wisdom

Wisdom is not mere wise words ...
Wisdom is not mere wise counsel,
Wisdom is not mere pearls of insight
Embedded in the discursive.

Wisdom is the crest of being ...
That luscious, silent fruit of
Days of endless contemplation,
Days of endless truthfulness.

Wisdom is the pealing crescendo of
Each virtue singing in the mind.
Wisdom is the supernal chorus of
All virtues ... integrated, integrating.
Wisdom is that hymnal choir,
The best harmony of all virtues that
Sprout like countless bouquets of
Fresh, fragrant flowers ...
Flourishing in the tender soil of the mind,
A garden of virtues nourished by
The blinding Light of the Infinite.

Wisdom is the silent, austere Doorway
Announcing the Supernal Light of the Divine,
Ushering It, welcoming It, propitiating It.
Wisdom is the River of Light, through which
Divine Light pours into each crevice of Consciousness ...
Illumining, decorating, until the mind, in its infinite calmness
Grows festooned with a radiant festival of Thought Lanterns.

39

Bridge of Justice

Of all the noble virtues, only Justice ...
A crown jewel ... appears to be born from
Roaring flames of anger.
For injustice spurs that anger, which
Makes man yearn for Justice.
All other virtues quell anger and other vices.
Only Justice, a virtue, appears to be born from a vice (anger).

But the search for Justice is not the same as
Reaching the equilibrium that *is* the virtue of Justice.
The abyss of anger spurs the search, not the goal.
Anger makes the search futile, for
Angry man moves from one node of injustice
To the next ... always touching Justice, yet missing it.
For anger is always unjust ... Even righteous anger
Runs the risk of missing the balance that *is* Justice.

Justice demands that we overcome anger.

Remote from anger
Stands Love ... a subtle flower.
Love is the balm that dissolves anger.
For Love surpasses, yet includes Justice,
Love being, at the very least, just,
Whereas, earthly Justice need not be loving.

No more than the grid that holds Love,
Earthly Justice forms the base
In the chalice of Love
That brims and overflows with eternal Light.

The search for Justice need not be loving,
Except for ...
The band of fragile ideological love
That binds the many against

Their common enemy ... the solitary tyrant,
In a temporary truce of altruism –
That first frail harvest of Revolution.

Justice is a divine Alchemist ...
A Powerful Bridge that transmutes darkness to Light ...
Even if injustice leaps out of the dark abyss of anger,
The thirst for Justice can adumbrate the virtue itself ...
And this anticipated virtue can end in Love,
If the semblance of Justice won is guarded carefully
By the Gardener who makes sure that
The frail petals of Justice blossom into
The power of Love in friendship,
A Love that transcends the need for rights –
So that the cry for Justice becomes redundant
In the hallowed portals of Love.

40

Garden of Virtues

This Earth is an ever changing garden
Visited by the seasons, now lush and green
With fresh reeds immersed in the marsh,
With a thousand flowers nodding in the wind
And chirruping birds celebrating
The keen felicity of Spring ...

This Earth is an ever changing garden
Visited by the seasons, now cold and bare,
With a thousand blinding, bleak snow drifts,
With the stamp of hibernation
And the escape of migratory birds –
The torpidity of the one balanced by the
Vigor of the other.

But in the swirling shining Heavens,
Beyond, yet within the peaceful Sky
And embedded in the center of the soul ...
There is a perpetual Garden
Nourished by the perennial Spring of Life,
Beyond Time and Space, yet within Time and Space.
For this noble Garden of Universals is
The abundant Garden of Virtues –
A no-man's-land that is every-man's-land,
For the Virtues belong to no one ...
They belong therefore, to everyone.
Eternal celestial gifts, they adorn the soul,
Relieving it of desire and sin, animating it,
Preparing it for union with the One,
Who rules this Garden of Virtues
Because It Exists beyond virtue and vice.

41

Worldliness, a Phantasm

The Worldliness of the World – a garish glare
Allures ... tempting man to dissipate himself ...
The bare eye sees it, the soul rushes to it,
As do moths towards their funereal pyre.

The Worldliness of the World emanates,
Not from our essence, nor from the world,
Even as it envelopes the world.
For, the world is not to blame for its worldliness.

This shimmer of phantom light,
Conjured, when we cleave to the unreal
As if cleaving to dreams ...
This glare is the beguiling fruit of attachments.
This glare is an alluring mirage that can entrap.
This wraith that mystifies our vision of the empirical world –
Granting false reality to the unreal –
This Worldliness of the World reaches beyond
The collective consciousness ... which is
A coat of many colors and the fruit of our collective desires.

The Worldliness of the World, an enticing halo ... is not evil ...
Neither good, nor evil, neither Being, nor non-Being
This phantom is not a progenitor, but an offspring of our desires.
It merely confuses, distracting us from the Supreme Light of Truth ...
The eternal Absolute, and the sole source of Being.

The worldliness of the world is a force of good,
When it is a distraction from corrosive anger.
This glittering mirage helps us escape ourselves
Away from the rumble of volcanic inner anger ...
Yet, it also adds to our stock of anger ...
If we get caught in the alluring net of worldliness,
We add to the dithyramb of anger
Already churning in the soul.

But when, like the fledgling plant, we hone ourselves –
Growing sharp and subtle in dispassion and discrimination,
Our desires grow pure ... receding with the receding ego,
And with the fading of desire anger fades and we begin to glow.
Enkindled with the new found Light of Gentleness,
We now can afford to dip into the sheer Worldliness of the World
Without intoxication, without drowning ...
For we now recognize this Worldliness for what it is ... a Phantasm.

42

Beauty Unleashed

The twig so frail, the distant star,
Slim drops of rain, a blade of grass,
Flying flocks of snow white birds,
Etched against the stone-gray sky,
Each compresses Beauty in the
Blind quivering matter of its frail body,
Surcharged with the ruthless
Animating power of Pure Beauty.

The Seer gazes beyond what meets the eye,
She sees the Transcendent shining through
The opacity of the Immanent.
She sees the Immanent visible in the
Invisible, ethereal Transcendent.
She sees the resplendent One
Appear as the prismatic many.
In Time and Space, in Being and Becoming
She sees the multitude of the teeming many,
Quivering within the Tranquil One.

The Seer, wide awake, is mesmerized –
Not by the miasmal glare of worldliness ...
But by the shining omnipresence of Truth ...
Our one and only Reality.

The Seer, wide awake, can see that
The Real encompasses the unreal
Surrounding it, bolstering it,
Projecting this miasma upon Itself,
Playing eternally with the temporal many,
Playing at the divine sport of hide-and-seek.

Beauty is the Light concealed in *all* forms ...
Those made of natural matter ... and man made forms,
For Beauty *is* the Real ...

Beauty *is* this divine Substratum that
Sustains the unreal it casts upon itself ... just as
The desert sustains the mirage it casts upon itself.

Gazing steadfastly into the theater of the many,
The Seer sees the Solitary One everywhere –
In the ornate sky, in the frolicking brook,
In moss laden stones,
Half dipping into laughing waters,
In the soft blue hills, veiled in conifers,
Frilling the wall of somber mountains –
Mute emblems of Opacity, yet alive with Spirit.

And everywhere she looks she sees
Nothing but the unifying presence of
Pure Beauty ...

Like a trembling shell, threatening to break –
Eager to release all struggling life,
Opacity struggles with silent tremors of
Its portion of the Light of Beauty ...
Threatening to erupt.
For this Beauty that transmutes opacity,
Will be contained no longer.

 "Beauty" that seals the eyes of the carnal beholder,
Rendering them opaque and blind ... is
A concupiscent distortion of Beauty Pure and Original.
It is a chimerical illusion that graces multiplicity,
Through shape, form, color, symmetry,
Each a graceful charlatan of Beauty Pure,
Each a potential trap of hatred.

But when the Divine descends,
Wearing the garb of Pure Beauty,
It vivifies the most misshapen, discolored,
Material objects, deemed "ugly" by the opaque eye,
For Beauty Pure is the Harbinger of Love ...
It beatifies by beautifying ...
By descending as one, but eliciting the
Manifold manifestations of Itself ...

For Beauty Pure elicits the Beauty Pure
Concealed and latent in all beings.

When a flood of Love arises in the heart,
Inundating, cleansing ... it appears as if
Love imbues Beauty Pure upon the Beloved,
Daubing paint upon a blank, paint-free canvas,
But this is only *seeming* ...

For Beauty Pure cannot be bestowed ...
It can only be elicited.
When a flood of Love arises in the heart,
Inundating, cleansing ...
It draws out the fire of Beauty Pure
Already latent in the Beloved.

Like the pearl concealed by its oyster,
Pure Beauty hides behind its
Veil of Opacity, seemingly leashed by
The opacity it projects as its
Garment of multiplicity.

But now, with seismic tremors of Love
Pure Beauty emerges,
Wrenching apart with bare hands,
Appearance from essence ...
Mingling the one in the unalloyed other,
Strengthening the opaque eye
Until it sheds opacity, becoming
Worthy of beholding
The all powerful, concentrated,
Untrembling halo of Beauty Absolute.

Like a hidden river bursting forcefully
Through hardened boulders,
The flood of Beauty, which
Will be stemmed no longer,
Bursts forth, renting to shreds its
Impassable veil of glittering opacity.

Beauty is the Song that rushes out of
The tethered silence of opaque multiplicity.

Chapter Seven

Time, Eternity, History

43

Time, a Snake

Time, a snake ...
Spits out of nowhere,
Vanishes into nowhere,
Moving forward ... ever forward.

A ferocious river, wedded to infinity,
In *duratio* and omnipresence,
Time leaps out of the dark tunnel of infinity,
Vanishes into the dark tunnel of infinity,
Its river bed, a dark Void of Infinity.

An ocean, heaving in one direction,
Color free, translucent ...
Its mammoth waves roiling and coiling,
Time drowns every creature in its home –
The graded heavens, hells, Earth – for
All is immersed in Time.

Inexorable, unappeased,
Time is a typhoon,
Blowing its conch in one direction,
Gathering the dust and grime of Immanence ...
Cleaning all with ruthless might.

A mirage made of thin gauze,
Time glistens with the fresh
Dew drops of History!
Like a cobweb, Time traps all.
Like a gossamer screen, Time filters
The blinding Light of its Pure Origin.
Like the moon, Time is
A moving sheet of lesser light.

Time, a roaring wave,
Erupts from infinity,

Erupts into infinity,
Leaping forward in thundering silence,
Cloaking the Divine by its antics.

Arrogant, merciless, Time presumes to be Divine.
Gliding over phenomena like a slithering snake,
Time appears like a mighty god.
Heartless witness of all that becomes
Time seeks to renounce Becoming ... but in vain.

In the end Time is an ember
Glowing amidst ashes of Creation,
Smoking and sullen, scorched unto oblivion.
For, when the blinding
Eternal Light of the Eternal One
Pours through Time, as
Experienced by the Meditating Mind,
It razes away the Cosmic Illusion,
Leaving behind nothing but
An infinite Void of sheer Radiance!

44

Nomadic Time, Motionless Death

Nomadic Time makes of us, natural wanderers ...
Not marching, but drifting, like drift wood.
The endless River of Time
Carries us on its rhythmic waves ...
We drift forward, ever forward ...

The shining Garland of Becoming
Threads together all beads of
Relative being, each bead embedded
In a resounding "now."
As we float on the nameless Tide of Time,
We are wayfarers, carried forward
Unwittingly ... unwillingly,
Carried by the Torrent of Time,
With Memory, the anchor to the past,
And Desire, the anchor to the future.
If Memory is the color we splash
On the canvas of the past,
Then Desire is the color we splash
On the canvas of the future.

As Time, the steward steers us forward
Trepidation steals into our hearts ...
Vagabond souls, we tiptoe forward ...
With dread.

For buried though we are in debris of desire,
We hear the muffled Call of Death ...
A crooning lullaby sung by
This silent, sapient Executioner,
A Sentinel, which guards itself as the
All ruling *telos* of the piece of Time we call life –
Visible, finite, chimerical.
Death, an amoral bower sings an amoral Song ...
A Song that pours down from nowhere ...

A Song that drapes us in its omnipresence.
For Death is ubiquitous ...
A gossamer Gateway,
Death leads from life to the afterlife,
Death is one, yet many.

The procession of life unfolds, propelling each being forward,
Towards the amoral, benign nemesis of
Its portion of finitude – its bodily, temporal lifestream,
Towards the white curtain of its unique, native Death.
Here it comes ... this magnificent Juggler,
Who juggles Time, Becoming, the *Karmic* Ledger, the afterlife –
We bow before this great Teacher,
We surrender before motionless Death,
We learn renunciation from Death.

45

Death, arm in arm with Time

Death, the Great Arbiter links hands with Time
To teach us humility ... we learn how to rest
In the infinite repose of Absolute Being
Concealed in the depths of each atomic "now"
Floating in the infinitude of Time.
For sitting inside the stealthy cavern of the "now"
As we meditate on the Divine Name
We pierce through Time to touch Eternity ...
We convert the garland of Time to a shining Rosary,
Its distention conjured by the Cosmic Illusion.
For Time is not real ...
Only the undying, unfractured Eternity,
Which is not a separate attribute
But the divine halo of Being Absolute ...
Only Eternity is Real.

Death, arm in arm with Time, teaches us
How to feign Becoming,
Anchored though we are to Being Absolute ...
By letting the melodious flow of atomic "nows"
That hold hands to form the Garland of Time
Carry us forward on its equal, undulating waves
Measure by measure, towards indifferent Death –
An Arbiter, which blows its conch shell,
Calling us to lose ourselves fearlessly
In its native Void.

Death and Time ... each perfectly amoral,
Yet they teach us the greatest morality ever.
Together, they slay Desire, purifying us
Until we emerge adorned with virtues ...
Forgiving, forgetful, desireless ...
Our memories polished into shining mirrors,
Cleansed of every darkening stain of anger,
Cleansed by the charitable hand of

Constant, spontaneous Forgiveness.
For the spinning wheel of Desire dragging us
Hither, thither, by the noose of our necks
Has been stalled forever.

The Mirror of Memory, now a moral compass
Allures the good soul to a final departure from Finitude,
Awakening it forever from opiating desires,
From the transmigratory cycle immersed in Time,
From the moral sphere immersed in *Maya*,
From the Cosmic Illusion.
Reaching beyond good and evil,
The Mirror of Memory hauls the perfected soul
To its final destination ... the bright Star of Eternity.
And what is this Being Absolute of Eternity,
But Reality Itself ... the infinite *telos* of all that becomes.

Like a dolphin diving joyfully in raging waters
The desireless good soul dives in the raging River of Time,
Dying perpetually, reborn perpetually, as it feigns Becoming ...
When all along it reposes in Being Absolute,
Having rent through the fleeting fabric of ghostly Becoming and Time.

Like the autumn leaf, whose beauty lies,
Not in the colors on the canvas of foliage,
But in its being the culmination of a life stream
That sums up the phases of the green leaf it once was ...

Like this autumn leaf,
Steadfast in its surrender to tender Life,
Which rushes headlong, like a heedless river, to
The thundering waterfall of Death, carrying with it
The unprotesting leaf, flinging this foliage over
The precipice of its unique, unshared Death ...

Like this autumn leaf, the good soul can be
A hoary fruition of a life stream.

Like a kaleidoscope jingling with colors
The good soul, which once jingled with thoughts,
Now moults the skin of old selves ...

These are to be revered, not wasted,
For each self was an oblation cast upon the
Pyre that exhumes sin ... a pyre aflame with embers of ethics –
A pyre that forges the good soul, making it blossom into the
Soul Flower that awaits Death by surrendering to Time ...

Equanimous!
Neither longing for, nor loathing Death,
The Soul Flower ascends the Ladder of Ethics by
Honing the virtues that erase evil ...
And once it surpasses the summit,
Reaching beyond good and evil,
It touches the bright Star of Eternity,
Rejoicing in its freedom from the moral sphere.
This supra moral Soul Flower now rents through
The illusive film of Death and Time –
Phantom gods in a phantom world.

Now powerful and free,
The Soul Flower tears through all contours of Immanence,
Piercing the ephemeral veils of Time, Death, Desire, Good, Evil,
Recognizing these Chief Sentinels, for what they are ... fleeting ghosts,
Touching the bright Star of Eternity, by reposing in Being Absolute,
Even as it rides the waves of Time that carry it forward
Towards the unique, unshared Death of its body ...
A phantasm in the phantasmal domain of *Maya*.

Free at last ... like the autumn leaf,
This now soul-free Soul Flower,
At once transcendent and immanent,
Throbs with Love
For it reposes *as* the Divine –
Being Absolute, Knowledge Absolute, Bliss Absolute.

46

Is Time a God?

Is Time a god?

Is Time one spark in
The shining constellation of divinities?

The Source is the full Divine ... a lone Reality.
The gods and demigods,
Luminous conduits of this Reality ...
Are now vivid, now faint.
For the shining spotlight of the One can sport
Through any god, goddess, or minor deity.

The Source is the full Divine ... a lone Reality ...
Total Light, trickling through the dimmer lights of
The gods and demigods.
Like the Ocean that hides its grandeur by
Trickling through rivers that draw from it,
Reality manifests Itself through celestial beings.

The Source is the full Divine ... a lone Reality ...
That hides Its glory beneath the
Opaque veil of *Maya*, which It projects
As Its dynamic Self, manifested in the act of Creation ...
Even as It sits still on Its Throne of Eternity,
Beyond relative being and Time,
Beyond good and evil.
Concealing Its static meditative Self,
Reality projects Its cascading, electric *Maya* to
Manifest the created worlds ... these are
Conjoint caverns hoisted by
Relative being and the mobile "now" ...

But this divine stillness erupts ...

Reality escapes now and then ...
Renting through the veil of opacity,

Shining Its spotlight here and there,
Manifesting Itself ... letting
One god express Its total Light,
Then another ... and another ...

Is Time among these gods ... ?
Does the Real shine through Time?
Is Time a concentrated theophany?
Is Time, a lower god ... a dilution of God as such ...
The full force of Truth – Our one and only Reality?

47

Kairos shining in Time

Like the omnipresent mast that
Holds together all visible worlds ...
Like the root that holds together the plant ...
Ubiquitous Time grips all relative beings,
Granting them ephemeral roots
In the Cosmic Illusion.

Like sea anemones and molluscs
Immersed in a translucent ocean,
All that journeys in the
Slow procession of Becoming –
The cosmos shining with orbiting orbs,
The graded heavens glowing in Time,
The graded hells glowering in Time –
All this is immersed in
The phantasmal, infinite *duratio* we call Time ...

Anything with relative being, is
Immersed in inexorable Time,
Both externally and internally ...
Although one, Time appears as two ...
The objective Time of physics external to us
And the internal Time, experienced subjectively ...
Whether external or internal,
Time is an unbroken continuum,
Flowing forward ... ever forever.

A scintillating river ... an infinite sequence,
Time glistens with flashes of fecund "nows."
Like scythes of Lightning that purify the sky,
A "now" flares here and there ... to form a living *Kairos* ...
A garland of purifying Moments of God ...
Contemplative Moments, Creative Moments ...

The River of Becoming is created when
Beads of relative being are threaded together
In individual strands of Becoming.

Like Rhythm, which melds with Music,
Like Thunder, which melds with Lightning,
Becoming melds with Time, to orchestrate
The living melody of relative being and Time,
The confluence of which equals Death.
Each relative being sits on its temporal throne of a "now,"
And each "now," a shining bead, bursts forth into the next
In an infinite sequence that vanishes like the morning mist,
When the all powerful One casts Its Total Light,
To ignite a glowing Requiem to Time.

Beginningless-endless, infinite in length,
Time cannot be captured, Time cannot be sculpted ...
Yet we seek to mold Time
In the petty grids of our calendars and schedules ...
In the petty gadgets of our clocks and watches ...

Trapping this Titanic Time in a calendar is like
Trapping the sky in a hot-air balloon or
Trapping the ocean in a bottle.

Uncoiling Time from its nest in the Divine
We seek to trap Time in these man-made molds
That rarely discern between
Moments of man and Moments of God
Moments mundane and Moments Celestial ...

The living *Kairos* threads together
Moments of God that shine like stars –
Turgid "nows" each brimming with Light,
Temporal garlands that form the living patterns of
Ideal seasons, both moral and prophetic.

Like water carving memories on unrelenting rock,
These living Moments of God etch
Upon the virginal soil of Time,
Quivering tracks of a Living *Kairos* ...
They are vessels for Epiphanies of Becoming –
Those special phenomena that express God ...
Those Golden Moments that do not interrupt
But punctuate the ceaseless flow of mundane "nows."
They designate those ideal and "right" times
Within the infinite, undulating Repose of Time.

48

Escaping Time

What is Time but a luminous, translucent Song ...
A celestial Song about its eternal Source ... Reality.

What is Time but a silent Sentinel,
Everlasting witness to the Receptacle of History ...
Objective enough to be scaffolded by calendars and clocks ...
Objective enough to be structured, uniform
And the same for every being ...
Yet, this singular Time is also subjective ...
Experienced by each being in a different way ...
And filled with the varying contents of varying life spans.

For every "now" is a sealed kaleidoscope
A moving vessel brimming with experience ...
Each "now" appears different in different lives ...
Some "nows" are wasted with the profanity of indolence
Like precious water wasted in a desert ...
Others are experienced with the purity that comes
From melding the lyrics of relative being to the tone of Time,
Choreographing this being to the hidden rhythm of Time,
In a celestial Song that combines the two, yet keeps them apart ...
Until they fuse in Death.
Some moments are elongated ... like the last "now"
On the brink of life, upon the shore of Death ...
Some flash by, seemingly a fraction of their objective *duratios* –
Like the idyllic "now" that drowns us in *Maya*,
Making us forget the passage of Time.

Every soul is vouchsafed that unique portion of "nows"
It wears like its garland of throbbing Finitude
To be severed by its unshared Death ...

But the best "nows" are those that part
Like gossamer curtains, to let us escape,
Through meditation, the illusion that is Time ...

A meditation that reveals these "nows"
In their ephemeral essence
And discloses Time as it is – a phantom Sentinel.

In the depth of meditation, when the great
Sun of Reality rises upon the sky-mind,
Like the morning sun rising in its full glory ...
It extinguishes all lesser lights ... among them, Time ...
As Reality banishes Its own prior mask of Time,
Each "now" parts like a shining curtain ...

Time vanishes as breath deepens, releasing us ...
Living sprites, we escape like wisps of wind ...
We escape the Phantom River of Time,
We escape to the living Truth that is the One –
The Being Absolute that inundates the procession of
All beings inundated in a seeming Time.

49

Awakening out of Time

Upon the waters of the Ocean of Time,
Countless linked life streams flow,
Each belonging to a tired soul,
Steeped in ignorance.

Bereft of Self-knowledge, this soul has succumbed
To the magic glare of worldliness ...
Endless wayfarer, she journeys from life to life
In the temporal transmigration of souls,
Unable to break through the thin film of Time,
By touching the all ruling Star of Eternity,
To free herself forever from
The desire-driven cycle of births, deaths, rebirths.

Each lifestream is linked to the prior and the next –
Each birth picks up from the death that ended the prior lifestream.
Each death leads ... after a bewildering temporal interregnum
Between two lives ... to rebirth in the next lifestream,
Whether on Earth, or in a graded heaven, or graded hell.
This entire caravan of cosmic life and acosmic afterlife –
A vibrant, colorful charade – is encompassed within
An unreal Time, ensconced in the rich miasma of an unreal
Becoming,
All this transpires on the silent loving bosom of the Absolute Real ...
Like an unreal convoy moving slowly, on an unreal stage,
Whirling in the dream of the divine Dreamer.

But when like a flare lighting a sooty lamp,
The all living Flame of Knowledge illumines a single soul
And one person escapes the Book of Time,
As this knower is uplifted, immersed, and dissolved
In noetic union with the supreme One ...
And as the libidinal drawbridge of knowledge
Is withdrawn forever ...
With the miasma of knowing conquered forever –

For knower and known have vanished like the morning mist –
This is when the eternal, amphibious divine Dreamer laughs
As It feigns sleep, beneath Its self imposed limiting veil of Time,
For, from among the slumbering many, It permits
Only one somnambulist to break free from
The shell of the divine Dream of Multiplicity.
The Dreamer allows only this one remarkable
Somnambulist to shed all garments of mortality
To awaken unto the divine consciousness of Itself
As the highest universal Self ...
The all ruling, vibrant, omnipresent One.

Like the rosy dawn that breaks out as a sun-drenched day,
This lone fugitive breaks out of the tentacles of the unreal many
Awakening in the recrudescent Light of the infinite One.

But nobody notices ...

Untroubled, the slumbering many remain asleep ...
Nobody notices the escape of one soul from the
Never ending Book of Time.
Nobody notices that from amongst the teeming created beings
A solitary soul has attained Self-knowledge ...
Awakening out of the dream of multiplicity,
Into its real nature as the silent, sapient One ...
Our one and only Reality.

Yet this golden escape impacts the slumbering many ...
Who tremble with the tremor of a ruffled multiplicity,
Like Earth trembles imperceptibly, in a small quake ...
Dissipating the enervating power of multiplicity,
The phenomenon of this celestial Escape,
Gleans the One out of the slumbering many,
Bringing all opiated souls, drugged with desire,
One step closer to the radiant knowledge of the One.
For mystical enlightenment, reached by escaping Time ...
Is neither solitary, nor self serving.

50

Traipsing through Time

The Sage sat on a white picket fence ...
Running from an endless past to an endless future,
Ever restless ... like a river flowing in measured laps,
Neither sluggish, nor rushing ...
For the fence was Omnipresent Time.
And sitting on that fence, riding with her
Was her kindred spirit – the entire Universe.

Like an obliging mare,
Time carried her forward on its back ...
And as she thus journeyed in Time,
The Sun rose and the Sun set,
And Earth orbited in her sacred dual orbit ...
Circle within graceful circle ... twirling on her tilted axis,
A self forgetful dancer, pirouetting forever,
Circumambulating around the Altar of the Sun,
In the ordered motion of steadfast contemplation.

When suddenly, before her bewildered eyes
The whole Spirit of Time dashed past,
Even though she was riding on Time.

What was this beautiful wraith?
It was Time ... a sacred Creature,
The drama of Creation concealed in its womb –
The pantomime of History ensconced in
The pantomime of the Universe –
Scenes of light, scenes of darkness,
Scenes that held the promise of transmuting
The bloodstained Slaughter Bench of History
Into a moral trajectory quivering with life ...
All this was revealed in the womb of Time.

And as the Sage sat still on that mobile Fence of Time
She saw the long streak of Time punctuated by

Periodic flashes of darkness and light,
A never ending necklace that threaded together
The multitude of days with the multitude of nights
And the Cosmic Days with the Cosmic Nights,
Each day promising its night
Each night promising the next day
All days and nights in the entire globe
Synchronized but not simultaneous.

And as the Sage sat still on that mobile Fence of Time
She saw the long streak of Time flash periodically
With the procession of the seasons ...
Every summer fading into winter,
Every winter brightening into summer,
All summers and winters in the entire globe
Synchronized but not simultaneous.

And as the Sage sat still on that mobile Fence of Time,
She saw the long streak of Time flash periodically
With the procession of a providential *Kairos* ...
Those Golden Moments of God that harmonize
Becoming with Time, erasing their usual strife
By providing a right Time for each happening.

Time was the Slaughter Bench, Time, the healer,
And Measureless Time it was, that
Allotted to each living being its ration of
God given, shared nows that illumined each life
With a portion of the living *Kairos*.
Like an underground river flowing beneath
The overt moments of each throbbing life,
Time, the Spirit, thus distributed itself
Without exhausting itself.

And Time it was that walked each soul
To its unique unshared Death,
Delivering the soul, into the hands of Death
But not abandoning it ...
For like a miserly money changer,
Timeless Death dealt in measures of Time,
Apportioning portions of finitude,

In rebirths on Earth or in the graded heavens and hells
All this immersed in the balanced, flowing finitude of Time.

And as the Sage sat still on that white Fence of Time
It was revealed to her that
She could hop off in the embodied state ... without dying,
For ... like shadows with no originals ...
Time was as unreal as the scenes that flitted past,
Scenes from History, scenes from the Universe.

In a sportive mood,
The divine Dreamer had
Inserted this illusory Fence of Time
In the middle of Its self-conjured dream,
To conceal Itself behind the gossamer film of Time,
And lend meaning ... granting purpose to Creation.

And as the Sage sat still on that mobile Fence of Time,
In the embodied state ... with Death held at bay,
A medley of echoes poured in ... echoes from
The collective Pantomimes of History, the Universe, the afterlife.
But soon all echoes faded before the splendor of golden Truth,
Rolling in with the surety of Music
Like a gust of air refreshing the woods.

For suddenly ...

The Sage vanished ... she was snatched
From her seat on that Fence of Time,
Snatched by the radiance of Eternity ...
The Truth that causes Time and its cacophony
To fade forever.

At long last, a hallowed silence ...
True quietude that transcends the discursive sphere,
Hushing forever the mirthless din of
Time, Space and Causality ...
Hushing forever, the noisy thralldom of thought.

51

Rosaries in Time

Unlike the Time of Physics,
The Time we experience is a snaking river,
But flowing forward ... ever forward,
Like railroad tracks, its framework linear,
With the sequence of "nows" intact,
The past always preceding the future ...
But its contents are designed by
A destiny forged jointly by the
Wild will of man and the steadfast will of God.

Unlike the linear Time of Physics,
The Time we experience is a snaking river,
Frothing, fuming with turbulent contents,
Meandering ... stumbling over
Giant boulders of History.

The oyster brews the shining pearl to perfection ...
The objective Time of Physics brews to perfection
The subjective hues of the Time we experience,
By letting eternal Contemplation flow through Time,
By harmonizing our Time with our clandestine
Relative being, as it unfolds through Becoming ...
All this before Death seizes being and Time
Fusing them in its own person,
For Death is the unity of the two.

Like seismic tremors stirring beneath rice fields ...
The smoldering contents of an erratic History
Stir beneath the measured surface of the Time of Physics.
The Slaughter Bench of History heaves sighs
Beneath undulating waves of objective Time,
Beneath this transparent stream of even tempered "nows"
Lapping past with the stealth of Night.

Yet ... amidst the flotsam and jetsam choking
The Time we experience, riding its measured waves,
Asymmetrically ... moving forward ... always forward,
There are a few rosaries of repeated thought ...
Each rosary traversing part of the trail of subjective Time,
Each repeated thought filling the cavern of a "now."
In fact, nomadic Time itself ... whether subjective Time ...
A stage that hosts the theater of raw human experience ...
Or the objective Time of Physics ... is nothing but a rosary ...
A series of identical, repeated "nows" dissipated and distended
Across the brooding, discursive "length" of infinitude.

But not all rosaries are equal ...

The delusional rosary of the Time that we experience
Hosts a trove of other brooding rosaries ...
Each defining a subjective state of soul ...
From the dithyrambic "rosary" of anger and hatred,
Repeating eerie echoes of churlish thoughts,
To the deceptive "rosary" of lust and greed
Repeating gluttonous thoughts, each
Obsessed with objects of pleasure.

Yet, these serpentine "rosaries" do not run amok ...
For they are ruled by a singular objective Rosary that
Bestows reality on the ghostly lower self ...
For the beads of this Royal Rosary
Repeat the Divine Name that blesses the soul,
Each bead, a droplet of incorporeal Light ...
Each bead, a droplet of undistended Infinitude ...
Mimicked in vain by the synthetic rosaries
Spawned by unruly desires and passions.
This archetypal Rosary ... this *Rosary* of all rosaries is
A sacrament of pure luminosity that spreads its aura of Truth,
Filling every "now" with its hallowed omnipresence.

As an Alchemist that defines
The purpose and essence of each life-span,
Revealing the divine nature in the creature,
This Archetypal Rosary traverses subjective Time,
Its dimension varying by the moral weight of the soul.

And as the pilgrim soul, evokes this royal Rosary,
Repeating the hallowed Divine Name, she pierces Time,
Transcending its subjective and objective aspects ...
Reaching salvation by touching the bright Star of Eternity.

Carried aloft by the Divine Name
Chanted within every temporal bead in
This Rosary of rosaries, saturated with Light,
The vigilant soul who repeats ceaselessly the
Life giving Name of God,
Conquers the buoyant Spirit of History by
Conquering her desires, passions and sins.

52

Time and Rebellion

Like a river that
Springs out of nowhere,
Springs into nowhere,
Omnipresent Time runs forever –
Sober, meticulous, ubiquitous.

Godlike in its equal dispensations of itself
Time is yet unlike the heavenly manna
Bestowed more on those who can receive more –
Time gives of itself *equally* to all and sundry.

Yet, even the objective Time of Physics is not a god ...
No more than the wraith that envelopes us
In the stream of Becoming,
Time is an amoral expression of Finitude.
Like the dream-like mist that envelopes nature,
Time is a dream we long to awaken out of.

Do we knock on the stolid Door of Time ... or ...
Does Time knock on the door of the soul?

As the Pilgrim Soul approaches the Absolute,
This Land of Light casts Its substantial Shadow –
A Real Shadow of the Real,
A veil made of Truth that veils Truth –
Upon the ascending Soul, revealing to her,
The dreamlike nature of Time.

Homeless, homesick, wistful, nomadic,
Nostalgic for our roots in the Land of Light,
We are caught on the treadmill of Immanence,
After meandering from life to life ...
We long for the Transcendent to resuscitate the Immanent.
We rebel against the blinding shutters of Time,
We rebel thus ...

In dismal ways through suicide ...
In celestial ways through Awakening.

Like fishermen trying to "catch" the ocean in fishing nets,
We seek to ensnare Time in our petty calendars and clocks.
But Time, ever noble, does not notice ... Time does not retaliate
When we who are loved equally by Time, mutineer against Time.

For steadfast Time loves us with unrequited Love ...
When Time corrodes the sphere of Immanence ...
Devouring the material world with zeal,
Time reveals Transcendence amidst Immanence,
Paving our way to the deathless Land of Light.
Time loves us ... but we are not grateful ...
We who pollute Time with heedless alacrity,
We who neglect Time by ignoring Death,
We do not love Time ... we revolt against Time.

For we, who are the children of Time,
Are yet, the greater children of Eternity.
Benevolent Time allows us to rend through
Its thin film of discursiveness ...
So that we may, at long last, reach salvation,
By touching the bright Star of Eternity.

53

Sunset and Eternity

Evening fell with quietude.
Night arrived like a thief,
To steal the last footprints of light.

The stealth and silence of Twilight
Indicates that other Great Silence –
The stillness with which Time unfolds,
Its Footsteps unheard, unheeded ...
Despite its infallible, relentless nature.

For, tranquil is the Night,
Tranquil is Time,
And tranquil is the soul who heeds both –
Time and that which Time indicates –

Unbounded, inimitable Eternity!

54

History!

Is History a cosmic joke ...
A Slaughter Bench whereupon
The gods toss their dice?

Or is History a random concourse of events ...
A blind ideal ... a cause that spawns
The slanted ethics of ideologies?

Or is History that irascible secular god
Who moves pawns from tryst to tryst,
Playing with the ebb and flow of events?

Like the tide uniting countless waves,
History is the coming together of multifarious actions –
Some consciously willed and freely chosen,
Others driven by the force of past tendencies and
Divine dispensations of the transcendental
Moral Law that jettisons events, forcing decisions.

Like ferocious waters licking black pebbles ...
The waters of History lick all human actions.
Like a turtle wading in the river,
History, a buoyant force, wades in Time
Carrying on its back, those that
Surrender to its *Zeitgeist*.

A confluence of myriad moral results –
Rewards and punishments decreed by the Moral Law
For actions in the current and all prior lives –
History is a sequence of related cosmic dramas
All immersed in a Cupful of Time ...
A kaleidoscope of characters plays roles
In the drama of History –
From the highest good, to the deepest evil,
And every shade in between.

Divine Justice is dispensed over the *duratio* of a
Dynamic Judgment Day, encased in the River of Time ...
Divine Justice is dispensed upon
A vibrant multihued meadow called History!

Myriad lives dip in and out of
This tapestry of colors we call History ...
Each life following the logic of its
Private course of Transmigration.
History is the flow of a million rivulets,
Countless currents of Reincarnation,
One enmeshed with the other ... like tangled veins,
Yet discrete ... each, an existential lifestream ...
Flowing near, oh so near,
Tempted to merge with the next and the next,
But thwarted by the barrier of the Existential Divide
That separates life from life.

History is the Spectacle conducted by
The Absolute Spectator upon Its divine bosom.
Solitary Wayfarer, the Spirit of History
Meanders in different guises
One in each manifestation of the universe,
Projected by the Divine, in the endless sequence of the
Cosmic appearances and disappearances of the universe.

Chapter Eight

Death

55

Requiem to Death

An ocean of change ...
Songbirds, trees, honey bees,
Mellow cows on meadows,
Fire leaping inside the cottage hearth,
Young mothers, their babies cradled,
Preparing Earth for another round of Bounty.

An ocean of change ...
Endless procession of the universe
In a whirl of multiplicity,
Its slow, linear march,
Its creeping motion ...
Imperceptible!

An ocean of change ... archiving transience,
Constant flux ... forward ... ever forward!

A convoy of change ...
Slow procession ... reeling with desire,
From tender youth to sagacity ...
From the freshness of Nascence
To the ripening of hearts,
Oscillating from desire to desire ...
From extreme joy to extreme sorrow.

An ocean of change ...
Flotsam, jetsam jettisoning down
The River of Life ... nonchalant!
Men, women, children, animals,
Trees, plants, forests, deserts,
The Slaughter Bench of History,
Stars and planets, orbiting orbs
A thousand Suns ... all this
Creeping forward in slow motion,
Immersed in the March of Time.

An ocean of change ...
But a futile metamorphosis ...
Futility itself! A dead end!
For this empty transition is

Bereft of a natural *telos*.
No fruition awaits this motion ...
No teleological reward justifies
The trillion travails encountered ...
Except the possibility of moral merit,
An undetermined potentiality that
Pertains only to Man and celestial beings,
In the order of Creation.
For all living beings are potentially divine ...
But only Man and the gods possess the free will
To kindle this dormant Light.

An ocean of change ...
Leading all and sundry to
The same yawning Chasm –
The Jaws of Death ...
That stark Precipice
Over which all must fall.

Good or evil, old or young,
Rich or poor, ill or well,
Monarch or serf, prince or pauper
Favoring none, disfavoring none,
Inexorable ... Death beckons all
With equal fervor.

We die but once ... yet ...
Death visits more than once.

When careening souls drag their bodies
Through the grime and dust of licentiousness
Through the ominous thirst for self injury
The Death Instinct flares up ...
Bellowing ... it smudges Infinitude with finitude,
Annihilating the moral yearning for Infinitude.
Before this bellowing Instinct
Death becomes a lust ... Death visits often ...

Therefore,
Death must be respected ... kept at bay ...
To speak lightly of Death is inauspicious,
To court Death ... is inauspicious,
To long for untimely Death is
The most inauspicious.

As the River of Time
Weds body closer to soul,
By erasing evil, with the brush of good,
Garnering wholeness and holiness ...
As Time thus transforms youth,
The lust for Death abates,
Even if with age, body and mind
Creep closer to natural Death.

Death must be worshipped
With incense and flowers
On the Altar of Renunciation ...
For next to God,
Death is the greatest Teacher.

Death must be worshipped for what it teaches –
Equality, justice ... for it spares nobody,
Forgiveness ... for it severs all enmities,
Renunciation ... for it denudes us of all
Likes, dislikes, possessions, friends, enemies
Mind, intellect, and the body.

The shadow of Death follows us
From the day we are born.
Eerie in its faithfulness,
It trails behind ... everyday.
Death derides us ...
For our folly in striking roots –
Seeking permanence on Earth,
Amidst ceaseless Transience.

The shadow of Death pierces into life
More than once –
Whenever body is cleaved from soul,
Because evil outweighs good.

The shadow of Death gathers form,
Looming large ... severe in its exactitude.
Unwelcome, untimely, unseemly ...
Suddenly, there it stands!

This Nemesis of Desire –
Death!

56

Death Purifies

Death is the grand sluice gate that
Regulates the countless orderly
Rivulets of Reincarnation,
Carved, decreed, and set in motion
By the law of Divine Justice.

Many and varied souls pass through the
Revolving doors of Death,
Which decimates attachments,
Turning these into ashes that yield
The glorious phoenix of Renunciation.

The closest of human bonds are
Rendered ephemeral, when
We reflect on Death *philosophically*.
For as the dying soul journeys forward ...
Its loves, its hates, its unholy indifference ...
All this grows dreamlike ...
Sundered forever, receding forever.

Before reaching Death ...
Or the interregnum between Death and Rebirth,
The dying soul is propelled by the self-willed
Momentum of its moral tendencies.
Like an arrow propelled by its impetus,
The dying soul flies towards new relationships –
The quality and identity of which depend on its
Prior attachments, desires, mental hankerings,
The moral tenor of its moral tendencies,
And the moral reparations it owes.

Father, mother, sister, brother,
Husband, wife, children, pets ...
No more than roles played,
Fictions that sustain us through

The lashing storms of life ...
They fade when the Grim Reaper arrives
They fade before the Gate of Death –
That abrupt, seeming
Consummation of the Play of Life.

Death purifies ...
Meditate on Death and all attachments –
Silhouettes and sources of oscillations ...
From specious pains to specious joys –
All this will give way,
To the Supreme Lone Reality of
Detached, egalitarian Divine Love.

Death purifies ...
Meditate on Death and the smokescreen will part.
Detachment distils each relationship,
Cleansing it of tainting contention.
Knowing the sheer finitude of mortality,
How can we quarrel ever?
How can we love ever?
How can we strike roots in a moving convoy,
Seeking permanence where there is none?

Death purifies ...
Meditate on Death, for it detaches us
From all gossamer threads of attachment,
Teaching us to reach the all shining
Immortality of Divine Love.

57

Precipice of Death

A roving voyage that can meander ...
Not randomly ... but endlessly,
The cycle of Reincarnation
Is not without purpose ...
It moves the self from life to life.
Blind and mute, the self is driven by
The momentum of its past desires,
Karmic dispositions, and the God given
Call to make *karmic* reparations.

The departing self, on its last journey ...
Stands carefully, balancing itself on
This acrobat's promenade –
The jagged edge of the Precipice of Death.

Swaying this way and that, the departing self sees
Two stark scenes, one on each side of this Precipice ...
On one side, an endless, undulating Valley of Memories ...
Rife with images of ancient loves, ancient hates,
Fireside stories, inspired moments,
All immersed in a Cupful of Time.

It dare not see the other side ...
The great "unknown" beyond Death ...
A tripartite Abyss – inhabited
First by the clamor of the graded hells,
And the sublimating heavens that quieten these hells ...
Second, by the whisper of future earthly lives ...
And third, by the scintillating Escape ...
That final Awakening from the unreal to the Real.

And as the departing self lurches,
Swaying on this final promenade on the
Sharp Edge of Death, it lets itself be pulled by
Delusive memories that tug at it ...

From the Valley below.
Like a miser, it rakes through memories,
In a frenetic search for virtuous deeds.

Once it finds these caches of acquired virtue
The departing self bundles them greedily,
Shaking off the dust from teeming memories ...
At long last, ready for its forward journey
Towards Death, the Nemesis of Desire.

What a lonesome journey ...
For nothing accompanies the departing self
Except the merit acquired by
The grueling practice of moral virtues and
The moral tendencies earned through good and evil actions ...
Dispositions that will prompt the departing self,
Granting it momentum and direction in future lives.

And with its heart wedded with its head,
The departing self ceases to falter ... for,
Having shed all fear, it turns forever from
The futile Valley of Memories.
With burning faith it turns to face
The thundering silence of the Abyss or
The Afterlife on the other side of the Precipice ...
The side that guards Time and can exceed Time.

Piercing through Time, in that
Single timeless moment before Death
What does the departing self see?

It sees ...
Shining beyond teeming future lives,
Towering above the plethora of
Desire laden heavens and hells, a
Great, luminous Void ... an emptiness
Bereft of names and forms of finitude ...
Bereft of every sin and desire ...
It sees ... the one and only Reality.

Spurning Time, Space, and Causality,
Brimming with self-surrender,
The departing self offers its last breath,
To this shining Void ... an oblation
For the sake of suffering beings.

Opening its bundle of virtues,
Slung carelessly on its shoulder,
The departing self scatters
All merit accrued from virtuous deeds –
It offers its merit in charity ...
Merit is now redundant,
For the Great Void ...
An all shining substratum of good and evil,
To be reached through the Abyss ...
Reaches beyond good and evil.

Then diving deep into the great Beyond ...
That shining, timeless Void ...
The departing self loses itself
In a final emptying of all finitude,
As it leaps into the one and only Reality.

58

Birth and Death

Like paper kites in the sky
They fly in florid colors ...
Countless pairs of opposites.

Like Cosmic Butterflies in Creation,
They fly in florid colors ...
Countless pairs of opposites.

Like fireflies mimicking stars
In the deep stealth of Night,
They fly in florid colors ...
Countless pairs of opposites.

Mysterious is the Night ...
Mysterious is its hum ...
Mysterious is the buzz of the opposites
Cascading from their Creator ... who
Creates them as the warp and woof of
The opaque veil of *Maya*.

Like constellations they congregate,
In the deep stealth of Night ...
Swarming pairs of opposites
Crowding the created worlds.

And among them ...
Birth and Death, Good and Evil,
Each pair holding hands in
The supernal parade of opposites ...

Together, Birth and Death
Kettle a lifespan ... yet ...

Birth and Death are not simple opposites ...
For although Birth is the death of fore-life
And Death, the birth of afterlife,
They are neither symmetrical twins, nor exchangeable ...
They are not simple, opposite Gateways into and away
From the stretch of Time we call "life" ...

Although each pair of Birth and Death is
The unique, exclusive existential fulcrum
That carves the life it gates from start to finish ...
As boundaries of this portion of finitude ...
Although Birth and Death are each an Existential Gateway ...
Although every Birth comes with its matching Death,
And every Death follows its matching Birth
Despite all this ...

Death is not a mere reflection of Birth upon
The relentless Mirror of Time ...
Death neither justifies nor explains the Birth
That begins the life it ends.

Yet Death can be
A distant echo of its matching Birth,
For we die as we live,
And we live in accordance with
The moral dispositions
That trail us from prior lives
Through the gateway of Birth.

For Birth is entrance
Into entanglement and desire,
Into opiating body consciousness,
Into the carnival of life,
Into self-deluding worldliness.
Above all, Birth is entrance
Into forgetfulness of life's original purpose –
Self-scorching search for salvation,
Desireless hunger for enlightenment,
Longing to awaken out of ordinary immanence
Into sheer Omnipresence and Omniscience.

Birth is the doorway to the mirage of Life,
Birth continues the cycle of Reincarnation,
Birth prolongs the state of ignorance,
Birth begins the state of conscious hypnosis,
Birth begins the mesmeric spell of Life.

Death is far greater ...

For Death can be a celestial aid to
Liberation through Enlightenment ...

Death can be a wrenching away
From every entanglement that enmeshes
The oblivious creature.
Death can be the Teacher who whispers
Words of deliverance to opiated beings –
Words that reveal the true nature of Life.

By parting the glittering curtains of worldliness
To reveal the True Light of Reality,
Death has the power to jolt us out of
The hypnotic grip of desire.

Birth does not possess the power to
Deliver man unto Eternal Freedom.
At best, Birth can be the gateway to a life
Teeming with myriad Moments of Atonement that
Lead up the shining stairway of virtue to
The enchanting Moment of Enlightenment ...

For Birth is caused by ignorance ...
By lingering desire, moral languor and
The moral ledger of past deeds that
Trap man in palpable meshes of
Desire, finitude, good, evil.

Death is far greater ...

Like a shadow enchained to its owner,
Death is enchained... not to Birth, but to Life.
Death shadows Life from start to finish.
But Death is an *independent* shadow, for ...
Death is not mere loss of Life
And Life is not the archetype of Death.
For Death possesses a substance all its own ...

Starting at Birth and traversing every moment,
This Supreme Limit and dark Shadow that is Death
Trails behind Life without pause ...
Death follows Life as its supreme Guardian of Virtue
Death follows Life as its supreme Guard of Time ...
Until the shadow triumphs, replacing its *seeming* master,
As Death replaces Life.

59

Death as Enlightenment

For the Sage
Death can be a final exit from Reincarnation –
A dying not merely to the body, nor to worldly life
But a dying through illumination ...
This supreme dying, an Awakening ... concealed, yet unconcealed ...
Asserts its presence only once ... when her cup overflows,
As she brims with meditative knowledge of God or Self ...
As much knowledge as is due to her,
As much knowledge as she can hold.

When this all shining crescendo of knowledge bears fruit
Upon the tender soil of her phantom lower self ...
When her power of knowing adumbrates Omniscience,
When amidst all this munificence, her unuttered propitiation of
Her inborn moral harvest is concluded,
For her lower self has died upon reaching the Summit of the Self,
Only then does the Sage hear the irresistible call of this glorious Death ...
To others Death may sound like the call of the wild,
But to the Sage the call of Death is the Call to Enlightenment.

When the day is done ...
And the sun sets on the horizon of life ...
The Sage reaches fruition ...
A sealed vessel of Grace, she is now complete and whole.
Fulfilling her matchless vocation on Earth,
She fulfills the universal purpose of her unique life ...
Availing of every occasion for redemption
Provided by the Great Redeemer ...
Riding on her frail lower self, until she reaches
The all shining universal Solitary Self.

Drenched in devotion, the Sage tarries no longer,
For the Cup of divine Grace overflows
As much Grace has been bestowed, as can be given ...
Fearless, steadfast, desireless ... whole and holy,
Immersed in the Soundless Sound

The Sage listens hard ...
She listens for that ultimate Death, a dying which is
Awakening as the One in the hallowed state of Enlightenment.

Spitting off body and mind
The Sage awakens through Death ...
She awakens from the dream of the unreal,
She awakens into the glorious Real,
She awakens *as* the glorious Real.

For the Sage,
Death is awakening.

60

Death Calls

When her past deeds have borne moral fruits
Stretching taut her translucent life,
When she has reached the rarefied summit of moral fruition,
When her self has moulted all prior silhouettes of itself –
Half formed, moth eaten monikers ... musty and obsolete –
When it has thus sacrificed its prior incarnations
At the altar of its highest teleological Self ...
When this great nameless, formless Captain of all lower selves
Has begun playing upon Its celestial flute, the special swan song,
Unique and native to her kinetic lower self ... none other,
When the Captain has played a message of awakening ...
Of release from Time and Finitude ...
When the Captain has played these plaintive notes oft enough
In the secret folds of her heart where these are audible in soft luring tones,
The Sage recognizes this swan song as meant for her ...
She know that Death calls!

61

Death, the Alchemist

Birth can be meritorious for what it brings about –
A series of "nows" brimming with the potential for redemption
But Birth, the abstract principle, is not necessarily meritorious in itself ...
Unlike Birth, Death itself can be commanding ...
Not merely the event of Death, but Death, the abstract principle,
Which is powerful to the soul that gains moral strength
By preparing for its departure ... by composing its own requiem.

How?

By worshipping Death
As the supreme check to all desire.

As the Great Alchemist, who converts the
Blatant finitude of life, to the finitude of the afterlife, or to
The time-free infinitude of the Luminous state of Enlightenment ...
An awakening that annihilates finitude,
As this Great Alchemist and Abstract Principle,
Death has the power to deliver the reflective self from all desire,
By infusing this kinetic self with a tincture of
The life giving, all consuming hunger for God.
Death can release us into the eternal freedom of Enlightenment ...
For we awaken thus, only when we die to the world.

Yet ...

How rare are those sparkling souls who thus prepare for Death ...
Departing like blazing meteors with festive flares of Joy,
Trailing their luminous virtues, in the wake of their freedom from fear ...
This freedom deriving from cosmic wisdom, Self-knowledge
And their perpetual ascent beyond good and evil,
To the luminous, immortal, norm-free vista of the supra-moral.

For those who thus die forever to the worldliness of the world
And triumph over every pair of opposites ... they alone are immortal.

Now Birthless and Deathless, they reach beyond good and evil,
Stepping into the ringing silence of the portals of Enlightenment ...
Having thawed every name and form in the
Fiery flames of Contemplation, emanating from the Divine,
They are finally free.

Only these released souls are
Worthy of Death ... the ultimate Liberator!

62

Every Road leads to Death

Every road leads to Death –
The humble trail through thorn and thistle,
The country road beneath the stars,
The snarling highway, ablaze with traffic ...
Every road leads to Death.

No bribing, or cajoling can stall
The determined footfall of Death –
The Grim Reaper arrives when he will ...
He is inexorable.

Death allows no baggage ...
We travel light when we die, carrying
Neither desires, nor possessions ... not even sins ...
Only the balance of merit and demerit
And a cache of moral dispositions.

Relentless Death ... so total ... yet unreal ...
No more than an actor in the Divine Pantomime,
This Sepulchral Sentinel is a phantasm that
Partakes of the Cosmic Illusion ...

Master of the unreal relative being
Ensconced in each "now" that flows
Through endless Becoming,
Immersed in the endless River of Time,
Death is also the Master Conductor that
Draws a symphony from the
Twin rivers of Becoming and Time –
Rivers that flow in unstoppable lifestreams,
Seemingly thwarted, seemingly halted, when
Dammed by the stolid Dam of Death.

Death is that time-free Sepulchral Magnet,
Neither temporal, nor eternal, yet,

A motionless confluence of Becoming and Time,
A confluence that transcends Becoming and Time.
Above all, Death is the ravenous executioner –
A solitary Sentinel suspended "forever" between
Illusory Time and Real Eternity.

Death, a ringing Hole in the Sky, has a diameter
Infinite in power, but of atomic *duratio* ...
Equipoised ... neither welcoming, nor rebuffing,
Death is majestic, silent, dignified ...
Death refuses all cloying attachments.

Like mountain rivers rushing headlong
To their dark, common cavern,
Heedless of doom,
Countless rapid life streams rush to
The gaping Mouth of Death,
Some attracted by
The active lust of the Death Instinct,
Others by the moral fruition of their deeds,
Each swallowed by ravenous Death.

Seemingly motionless,
Yet this gleaming Hole of Death is unquiet ...
Death, an illumined ring, whirls ceaselessly ...
Death whirls with the kinetic power of
Unfulfilled desires.

But to those who have labored to ignite the
Flaming pyre of Renunciation,
Expunging the Death Instinct,
Offering every fluttering desire
As oblation and ember to this smoking pyre –
To this special being,
Death is the shining halo of Peace Eternal.

To those who have surrendered
All possessions, thoughts, desires, deeds
To the Divine, which uses
The sepulchral ruse of Death to win back souls
So lost in the mire of worldliness –

To those special beings,
Death is the quiet halo of Peace Eternal.
To them, this same gleaming Hole of Death
Is a wide open window that lets in
The supernal sunshine of the Divine ...
A Light that refreshes and illumines
All that becomes with
The undying power of divine Mercy.

Death brooks no idle chatter about itself.
Death must be wooed in silence ...
Death must be propitiated by
Immolating unto oblivion every sin, every lingering desire
Upon the smoldering Pyre of Renunciation
Ignited by Death, stoked by nomadic Time.

63

Death Purified

When polluted by the shadow of lust,
Death distorts its tone, enunciating itself
As the Death Instinct that flares aloud –
A fatal magnet that traps souls
In their untimely Death through suicide ...
Like the candle flame that is
Profaned when used for arson,
Death is profaned in suicide.

But when the Light of the supreme One
Wrings Death dry of the shadow of lust
And blesses Death with its own Delight,
The Death Instinct wanes ...
Before this high tide of Life,
Before this supreme self surrender,
Death itself becomes hallowed ...
Inspiring, not fear, but the unending
Exhilarating Joy of true Freedom.

64

Death was a Friend

Down the clairvoyant River of Time
The Sage floated in her raft ... an atomic "now"
That strode the rough eddies of a measured Time,
Flowing forward ... ever forward.

Down the clairvoyant River of Time
The Sage floated in her atomic raft,
A mobile witness, feigning stillness.
Tucked snugly inside the "now,"
She watched other lives and lifespans
Pass by like unreal dreams witnessed by
This somnolent dreamer, unaware that
Her real Host ... our one and only Reality,
Was the Eternal Spectator within ... or
The luminous Self that commands Time.

Down the clairvoyant River of Time
The Sage floated in her atomic raft ...
Cleaving to this measured "now,"
Heading towards her unique, indifferent Death,
That ephemeral sluice gate that chops off life.

Down the clairvoyant River of Time
The Sage floated in her atomic raft ...
Terrified of Death –
A parsimonious Executioner
Who slices in pieces the never ending
Temporal infinitude of Time ...
A miser, who doles out,
Fragments of finitude ... with seeming caprice.

Down the clairvoyant River of Time
The Sage floated in her atomic raft ...
Alert to the call of this brutish brigand –
Inexorable Death ... which will

Rudely snatch at the frail raft of
Her nomadic "now," tossing her off course,
Devouring the "now."

But when the Sage finally arrived,
Ever courteous Death reached into Time
Steadying with its own hands
The delicate raft of her "now."
Playing with Time ...
Shaking the kaleidoscope of her Past and Future,
Death cast both in the Light of Truth,
Letting the power of her
Purified memory atone for her sins,
Purified imagination free her of the future.

And with this,
Death devoured her desires and sins,
Steadying her raft of the temporal "now"
Devouring the "now" itself and
Her potential entrapment in Time,
Through never ending cycles of transmigration.

Death helped the Sage escape the multitude of
Her potential lifespans, caught in
The never ending Treadmill of Time,
Like the multitude of Times are caught in
The never ending Treadmill of Becoming.

Like a faithful Sentinel,
Death delivered the Sage
Beyond the limits of finitude,
Unto the hallowed portals of Eternity,
Her eternal Universal Self actualized in the
Blinding Light of Truth that
Delineates Eternity.

For ... Death was a Friend.

Chapter Nine

Nature

65

Pilgrims in the Sky

Saffron blush upon fading blue,
Saffron trail of setting Sun ...
Fiery Monarch sprinkles rosy petals of light,
To etch its parting for the day, smearing its path
With saffron laced clouds, aflame with the
Blood stained light of the fading Sun.

Ignited fringe of every cloud shines
Like a live ember of ash smeared coal ...
Clouds with rosy rims shine like
Signatures of the sanguine Sun,
Fading fast upon the quiet sky-sea –
An ocean, throbbing with numberless
Glistening crystals of Joy that vibrate ceaselessly,
Throbbing beneath the delicate translucent
Fabric of the saffron-blue sky –
Crystals of Joy manifested as the subtle
Celestial Light that animates corporeal light,
Pouring through the delicate translucent
Fabric of the saffron-blue sky.

Saffron melts to fading blue,
Saffron mingles with fading blue,
In the tender shine of
The saffron-blue stripe of sky
That separates gently
Saffron from sky blue.

Above this band of illumined saffron-blue
A solitary jewel shines ... lone majestic star
Rules the endless sky-pastures,
A radiant clue to the Divine Light
That shines through the porous screen of the twilit sky.

One lone star ... a luminous window into
The blinding celestial Light, ensconcing this universe ...
A Light that reaches well beyond
The native halo of our native cosmos ...
For It is that Infinite Radiance ... a blazing Fire of Love,
We call our one and only Reality.

Like a Ball of Fire that nurses
A ghostly black hole in its womb,
This Fire of Love,
This Fire of Life,
This Fire that is Reality
Ensconces in its womb,
The black hole of the empirical world ...
A Cosmic Illusion.

Like a team of oars ...
Synchronized in concerted motion,
Lapping in rhythmic splashes ...
A flock of wild Canada Geese
Fly joyfully, in the living pattern of
A dark, fluttering arrowhead –
A flying signature swimming gracefully
Across the glowing sky.

How natural they look ...
These grand Natives of the Sky
As they move in chiming motion,
Rowing across the yielding sky,
Crying in chorus ...
Their clamorous honking ...
A mysterious adoration of the Divine,
Which for them, is the infinite saffron-blue sky.

Like pilgrims, they cross this divine terrain,
In their ritual flight from winter.

66

Changing Seasons

Dappled leaves sail to the ground,
Dark brown acorns roll on the grass.
These minstrels of Nature
Proclaim to all who will listen ...
The blithe arrival of Autumn.

Flaming yellow, orange, brown
Have stolen from the leaf
Its subterfuge of summer green ...
Nonchalant clouds hail the skies,
Migratory birds sail the skies
Honking their way to warmer climes ...
Like misers hoarding gold
Squirrel, chipmunk, and the rabbit gray
Store their stock of winter nuts and acorns ...

Soon the boughs will be bare
Like Truth revealed before starving eyes,
As winter arrives with the majesty of
Blinding snow drifts.
Bare branches will lift their unadorned arms
Shorn of every trembling leaf ... they will
Portray the grace of their ascetic tree.

Like the austere snow-laden Bough,
Like the austere snow-laden Sky,
Like the austere snow-laden Earth,
The eye now austere, will draw beauty from the
Starkness of the arcane tree
Offering its boughs in adoration
To the cracked, marble, unrelenting sky,
Laden heavy with unshed snow
Like eyes filled with unshed tears.

The eye now austere, will seek beauty in that
Which it never noticed before –
The naked shape of the tree, its visible silhouette,
The pose it strikes ... like a delicate dancer,
The intricate pattern of its interlacing boughs
Offered in homage to the flinty sky,
Craving alms from the flaccid Sun,
Praying for the return of a bountiful Spring.

This merry-go-round of Nature, its change of seasons,
Is really the revolving Stage where the unchanging Constant –
The nameless Divine One – switches masks as It beguiles
The unknowing eye with its myriad disguises.

For ... our one and only One is a shining chameleon,
Changing costumes by changing the seasons ...
The One mystifies the world, lost in Original Sin,
Bemused in a cloud of Original Unknowing
A state from which the world awakens,
When the One unleashes its divine potential.
The world awakens further, when we
Recognize the One in the state of nature
And worship the shifting scenes ...
Beholding the changing seasons as Vessels of Grace ...
Living Icons of Blinding Light, about to spill forth
The hallowed contents they can barely contain.

67

Autumn

A gentle breeze arrives ...
Soothing visitor,
It brings joy to a troubled world.
Refreshing zephyr,
Life giving Breath of God,
It brings glad tidings and tranquility.

Ten thousand leaves sail across in a slant,
Riding the crest of a jubilant breeze.
Aflame with color ...
Rusty red, orange, yellow-green ...
They swirl in circles, with abandon ...
Like children playing on a merry-go-round.

Ten thousand leaves blow across,
Ungrieving in their final departure
From the parent tree, which
Nourished them yearlong.
Ten thousand leaves blow across
With nonchalance,
Like pilgrims, flowing with faith,
Unconcerned of their final destination ...
For it is not the bleak snow that awaits them,
But the gentle lap of Earth.

The Sage sits by the window ... and through
The fronds of snow white curtains
She sees ten thousand leaves sail by,
Drifting restfully, upon the wings of
The gentle breeze they trust ...
Each leaf, an epistle of the Divine Name.

68

Tree Alchemy

The Sky, a rugged Cloud-Quarry,
Etched with aerial stones ...
Flinty fields of curling clouds,
Silver, white, smoky-gray,
Gentle blue, tinted red.

Like molten lava –
Steaming treacle of Life,
Coiling down the hillside –
These beautiful billowy clouds
Meld one into the other,
Roiling and coiling,
Turning the dank Sky-Canvas
Into an opaque, churning fortress.

Like the meadow that conceals dark, fecund soil,
This Cloud-Quarry conceals the fecund Sun
Which shines forth, through its Cloud-Veil,
A veritable veil of *Maya* ...
How high It whirls, this Fiery Whirlpool,
Our Sun of Contemplation ...
Rejoicing in Itself, coiling endlessly,
Churning with centripetal power,
Absorbed in majestic motion ...
Tranquil in Its mystic absorption,
Emitting ferocious flames of Contemplation,
Deepening the silence of the dying day.

A skeletal copse ... trees, burdened by
Their fair share of snow, congregate in the
Stark silence of the tender evening,
Their amiable treetops leaning together,
Beneath the glowering flinty sky.
They are conjoined by the supreme
Breeze of Amity that descends from above –
A bounty bestowed by the Flaming Sun.

Black tree branches, lined white,
Etched against the flinty Sky,
Drip with soggy snow ...
Their interlacing boughs frame the Sky
Like latticed windows fragment the
Infinite Sky in finite Sky pieces.

Every bald tree, shorn of foliage
With arms upraised, in prayerful praise
Is a beautiful form, a sculptured candle,
Its canopy of bare boughs
A frozen latticed flame.

Every bald tree, shorn of foliage
Makes a gift of its inmost essence
Blessing the eyes that behold its form,
Filling the heart of the viewer
With its greatest treasure –
Its Tree Essence.

 Every bald tree, shorn of foliage
Overflows with a
Seemingly finite Tree Essence ...
What can this essence be, but
The infinite Essence of Beauty –
Unchanging, eternal, Divine Beauty ...
Beauty that is Faith itself,
For the Tree's silent loveliness
Drawn from above, impressed upon its
Gnarled outer form of bare interlacing boughs
Imbues the eye with the
Healing, life saving salve of Faith.
What is this silent balm of Faith, but
The Gateway to pure Devotion.

Every bald tree, shorn of foliage
With arms upraised, in prayerful praise
Is a force of Divine Alchemy
For through its multiple powers –
Meditative stillness, natural grace, charity –
Each Tree transmutes

Its borrowed power of throbbing Beauty into
The living Power of Faith.

And through the opaque screen of
Flinty clouds, the Sun emits
Quivering rays of Life, each ray,
A subtle Epistle of the Divine Name ...
A Name that curtails multiplicity,
Threading the unreal many into
Our one and only Reality.

Each ray of the Sun animates
The Sky, the Clouds, the Trees ...
Until the host of trembling Trees
Chorus in silent tones, as they
Join hands to unleash the
Leashed Power of the one unique
Essence of Beauty they partake of,
Communally ... alongside every life form,
Like a thousand rivers drinking from the
Same inexhaustible ocean.

This solitary Power of Beauty, now unleashed
Floods a stricken Earth, famished with cynicism.
Its inundates Earth with the abundance of
Faith that lay frozen within each tree
As its inmost Power of Beauty.

For Faith when dormant, is Beauty
And Beauty is Faith in potentiality ...
The Essence of Beauty is the Seed of Faith.

69

Sky Sacrificed

Slowly they move, Dark Potentates,
Gray flotilla of determined Clouds,
Graceful procession, roiling, coiling,
Inching forward, with menacing purpose,
Propelled by unwilled laws of Nature,
Decreed, but never determined ...
For, although commanded by Nature's laws,
They are free ... relishing their inner wild.

Every being in Nature is alive, ensouled,
Enslaved to none, radiantly free.
Each leaf obeys the wind, yet remains free.
Each flower obeys Nature, yet remains free.
Any being, which trembles with Life,
Also trembles with Freedom,
To be Alive is to be Free ...
For the Life that vivifies, also frees ...

Archangel of Alchemy, Life animates by
Bequeathing itself, infusing intelligence into corpses,
Enlivening each ... For Life itself is freedom.

Not mechanical, yet inexorable,
Nature's laws never demand
Blind homage from Nature's creatures.
Even Rain Clouds know they must cleave
To the Divine Talisman of their inner wild,
Never relinquishing, their inmost freedom.

The wilderness cannot be tamed.
Nature's laws *guide* her thousand creatures,
Neither incarcerating, nor domesticating.
Nature alone has the wisdom to harmonize
Freedom with necessity.
Nature's creatures roam unchecked,
Disciplined, yet wild ... ruled, yet unruly.

But this freedom is of a lower order ...
It is a relative freedom ... amoral, untamed ...
It is a relative freedom ... unthinking, ungoverned ...
It is a freedom from conscious willing.
Nature's creatures obey blindly
The more mechanical rules of nature ...
For they are oblivious of rules that entail free will.

This secondary, relative freedom ... relished by
All sentient and insentient creatures (barring Man),
Is therefore ... a strange freedom that
Incarcerates thinking Man, to a greater degree than
All encroachments from Nature's rules.

Even as he obeys Nature's rules,
Man must struggle against this secondary freedom
In Nature's creatures ...
Man must struggle against his own unruly lower nature,
By sublimating it through moral discipline ...
For man alone is capable of the highest Freedom ...
A total, ultimate Moral Freedom,
Earned by a grueling conquest of his lower self.
The call of the poet, and all the living arts,
The magnificence of Nature, Man's own inner yearning ...
And above all, the saving Grace of the One,
All these, especially the last, enable Man to ascend
From relative freedom to
The supernal glory of True Freedom.

Nature contributes ... by offering supreme oblations
For the good of Man ... her Chief Steward ...
She makes sacrifices for the sake of
Man's moral emancipation ...
A liberty with cosmic import.

Slowly they move, Dark Potentates,
Wild thunder Clouds, brimming with rain,
Ash-gray billows, ever obedient to the
Lawbound call of Nature ...
Yet their first allegiance remains with the
Divine Call of their inner Wild.

The sky broods ...
A majestic rumble hints at Thunder.
Treetops sway, their foliage distracted.
A thousand leaves tremble at the coming of the Storm.
The squirrels have vanished, soggy birds hide in clusters,
Their wings dripping rain.
The distant willow droops lower and lower.
Swirling mists cascade on Earth, as a sheet of rain descends,
Each drop of moisture suddenly glowing in the light of
A sharp streak of Lightning that ignites the darkness
To illumine its Bloodless Sacrifice of the infinite Sky.

For Lightning will conceal nothing ...
Ruthless, beautiful ... an Embodiment of Truth,
But also the very essence of everything wild,
This thin, quivering Line of Light, a celestial knife,
Flashes out ... suddenly ... dangerously
To plaudits of Faithful Thunder,
As Lightning tears the trembling Sky,
Cleaving apart in a savage moment,
The infinite Sky into finite Sky-parts,
Revealing the hidden heavens ...
Then vanishing ... like a coy *prima donna*.

Awestruck ...
Man pays homage to a Sky strangely sutured ...
After being sacrificed upon the ruthless Altar of Nature,
All for the sake of Man's redemption.

Chapter Ten

Postlude

Divine Mother

An Ode to Goddess Durga

Oh divine Mother of the Universe,
Magnificent in your bearing,
Opulent in your mercy,
You inspire awe –
Astride your lion with the golden mane,
Its teeth baring ferociously.

Your dark, thunderous hair
Cascades through the stars,
Your regal smile combines benediction
With the power to strike terror,
For you relate to your creation
In three separate ways –
You rule from beyond good and evil.
Yet you are also the divine substratum of
Good and evil.
But above all, You manifest yourself
As the Kernel, in forms both good and evil.

Your gaze, firm and tender,
Your upraised arms, ten in number,
Your form made of the
The secret might of Reality –
A Reality that imprints its matchless force
Upon the nebulae of the unreal ...
All this promises eternal freedom from fear.

At once, Benevolent and Terrible,
You are ubiquitous,
With a seeming ubiquity
In the mirage of multiplicity.

Oh ten armed Goddess ...
Bejeweled and ornate, of golden hue,
Your Third Eye radiates rays of knowledge
From the middle of your sky like brow.

Oh divine Goddess ... your upraised arms
Ten in number, dispel fear –
They shower blessings that fall like
Flowers upon a stricken Earth.

Oh majestic Goddess ...
With your upraised arm,
With your mighty spear,
You pierce the heart of evil.
Every demon shudders in terror,
Each flies helter skelter ...
Evil scatters, dissipating itself
In the brilliant, molten
Light of Good you pour forth
From your munificent Eye.

Index of Poems in Alphabetical Order

Index of Poems by Number and Date

43. Time, a Snake, July 10, 2009
44. Nomadic Time, Motionless Death, Sep 12, 2010
45. Death, arm in arm with Time, Sep 22 to Oct 31, 2010
46. Is Time a God? Sep 22 to Oct 31, 2010
47. *Kairos* shining in Time, Sep 22 to Oct 31, 2010
48. Escaping Time, Sep 22 to Oct 31, 2010
49. Awakening out of Time, Jan 15, 2011
50. Traipsing through Time, Dec 25, 2011
51. Rosaries in Time, Feb 9, 2011
52. Time and Rebellion, July 20, 2011
53. Sunset and Eternity, Apr 25, 2011
54. History! May 19, 2009
55. Requiem to Death, Feb 12, 2009
56. Death Purifies, May 22, 2009
57. Precipice of Death, July 5, 2009
58. Birth and Death, Dec 15, 2010
59. Death as Enlightenment, Dec 15, 2010
60. Death Calls, Dec 15, 2010
61. Death, the Alchemist, Dec 15, 2010
62. Every Road leads to Death, Dec 30, 31, 2010
63. Death Purified, Jan 16, 2011
64. Death was a Friend, Mar 16, 2011
65. Pilgrims in the Sky, Sep 11, 2010
66. Changing Seasons, Sep 26, 2010
67. Autumn, Oct 10, 2010
68. Tree Alchemy, Dec 25-26, 2010
69. Sky Sacrificed, Sep 3, 2011
70. Divine Mother, Sep 12, 2009

The Prometheus Trust Catalogue

Platonic Texts and Translations Series

Iamblichi Chalcidensis in Platonis Dialogos Commentariorum Fragmenta (*John M Dillon*)
The Greek Commentaries on Plato's Phaedo I – Olympiodorus (*L G Westerink*)
The Greek Commentaries on Plato's Phaedo II – Damascius (*L G Westerink*)
Damascius, Lectures on the Philebus (*L G Westerink*)
The Anonymous Prolegomena to Platonic Philosophy (*L G Westerink*)
Proclus Commentary on the First Alcibiades (*Text L G Westerink Trans. W O'Neill*)
The Fragments of Numenius (*R Petty*)
The Chaldean Oracles (*Ruth Majercik*)

The Thomas Taylor Series

Proclus' Elements of Theology
Select Works of Porphyry
Collected Writings of Plotinus
Writings on the Gods & the World
Hymns and Initiations
Dissertations of Maximus Tyrius
Oracles and Mysteries
Proclus: The Theology of Plato
Works of Plato in five volumes
Apuleius' Golden Ass & Other Philosophical Writings
Proclus' Commentary on the Timæus of Plato in two volumes
Iamblichus on the Mysteries and Life of Pythagoras
Essays and Fragments of Proclus
The Works of Aristotle in nine volumes
Dissertation on the Philosophy of Aristotle
Proclus' Commentary on Euclid
The Theoretical Arithmetic of the Pythagoreans
Pausanias' Guide to Greece in two volumes
Against the Christians and Other Writings

Students' Edition Paperbacks

The Sophist
The Symposium
The Meno
Know Thyself – The First Alcibiades & Commentary
Beyond the Shadows - The Metaphysics of the Platonic Tradition (*Guy Wyndham-Jone. and Tim Addey*)
The Unfolding Wings - The Way of Perfection in the Platonic Tradition (*Tim Addey*)

Other titles

Philosophy as a Rite of Rebirth – From Ancient Egypt to Neoplatonism (*Algis Uždavinys*)
The Philosophy of Proclus – the Final Phase of Ancient Thought (*L J Rosán*)
The Seven Myths of the Soul (*Tim Addey*)
Release Thyself – Three Philosophic Dialogues (*Guy Wyndham-Jones*)
A Casting of Light by the Platonic Tradition
The Song of Proclus
Platonism and the World Crisis (*John M Dillon, Brendan O'Byrne and Tim Addey*)
Towards the Noosphere – Futures Singular and Plural (*John M Dillon and Stephen R L Clark*)
An Index to Plato

For further details visit www.prometheustrust.co.uk